Y0-CBH-786

MACMILLAN McGRAW-HILL
Science

Lucy H. Daniel

Jay Hackett

Richard H. Moyer

JoAnne Vasquez

About the Cover

Chameleons are known as the masters of camouflage. They have the ability to change their skin color and patterns. Chameleons are slow-moving animals so they rely on protective coloration for defense. For protection, a chameleon might show bright colors, which often means "bad-tasting" or "poison" to predators. If this doesn't work, they may shift to a dull color and play dead.

INQUIRY **What else would you like to know about chameleons? Write your own question or questions to answer.**

Macmillan
McGraw-Hill

Program Authors

Dr. Lucy H. Daniel
Teacher, Consultant
Rutherford County Schools, North Carolina

Dr. Jay Hackett
Professor Emeritus of Earth Sciences
University of Northern Colorado

Dr. Richard H. Moyer
Professor of Science Education
University of Michigan-Dearborn

Dr. JoAnne Vasquez
Elementary Science Education Consultant
Mesa Public Schools, Arizona
NSTA Past President

Contributing Authors

Lucille Villegas Barrera, M.E.d.
Elementary Science Supervisor
Houston Independent School District
Houston, Texas

Mulugheta Teferi, M.A.
St. Louis Public Schools
St. Louis, Missouri

Dinah Zike, M.Ed.
Dinah Might Adventures LP
San Antonio, Texas

The features in this textbook entitled "Amazing Stories," as well as the unit openers, were developed in collaboration with the National Geographic Society's School Publishing Division.

Copyright © 2002 National Geographic Society. All rights reserved.

RFB&D
learning through listening

Students with print disabilities may be eligible to obtain an accessible, audio version of the pupil edition of this textbook. Please call Recording for the Blind & Dyslexic at 1-800-221-4792 for complete information.

The McGraw·Hill Companies

Macmillan McGraw-Hill

Published by Macmillan/McGraw-Hill, of McGraw-Hill Education, a division of The McGraw-Hill Companies, Inc., Two Penn Plaza, New York, New York 10121.

Copyright © 2005 by Macmillan/McGraw-Hill. All rights reserved. No part of this publication may be reproduced or distributed in any form or by any means, or stored in a database or retrieval system, without the prior written consent of The McGraw-Hill Companies, Inc., including, but not limited to, network storage or transmission, or broadcast for distance learning.

FOLDABLES is a trademark of The McGraw-Hill Companies, Inc.

Printed in the United States of America

ISBN 0-02-282606-8

5 6 7 8 9 058/043 09 08 07 06

Teacher Reviewers

Michelle Dunning
Birmingham, Alabama

Donna Bullock
Chandler, Arizona

Debra Allen
Davie, Florida

Lora Meade
Plantation, Florida

Roxanne Laird
Miami, Florida

Karen Gaudy
Satellite Beach, Florida

Stephanie Sirianni
Margate, Florida

Heidi Stephens
South Daytona, Florida

Rosanne Phillips
Miami, Florida

Brenda Crow
Miami, Florida

Kari Pingel
Pella, Iowa

Christie Jones
Springfield, Illinois

Diane Songer
Wabash, Indiana

Lee Arwood
Wabash, Indiana

Margarite Hart
Indianapolis, Indiana

Charlotte Bennett
Newburgh, Indiana

Donna Halverson
Evansville, Indiana

Stephanie Tanke
Crown Point, Indiana

Mindey LeMoine
Marquette, Michigan

Billie Bell
Grand View, Missouri

Charlotte Sharp
Greenville, North Carolina

Pat Shane
Chapel Hill, North Carolina

Karen Daniel
Chapel Hill, North Carolina

Linda Dow
Concord, North Carolina

Consultants

Dr. Carol Baskin
University of Kentucky
Lexington, KY

Dr. Joe W. Crim
University of Georgia
Athens, GA

Dr. Pradeep M. Dass
Appalachian State University
Boone, NC

Dr. Marie DiBerardino
Allegheny University of
Health Sciences
Philadelphia, PA

Dr. R. E. Duhrkopf
Baylor University
Waco, TX

Dr. Dennis L. Nelson
Montana State University
Bozeman, MT

Dr. Fred Sack
Ohio State University
Columbus, OH

Dr. Martin VanDyke
Denver, CO

Dr. E. Peter Volpe
Mercer University
Macon, GA

Consultants

Dr. Clarke Alexander
Skidaway Institute of
Oceanography
Savannah, GA

Dr. Suellen Cabe
Pembroke State University
Pembroke, NC

Dr. Thomas A. Davies
Texas A & M University
College Station, TX

Dr. Ed Geary
Geological Society of America
Boulder, CO

Dr. David C. Kopaska-Merkel
Geological Survey of Alabama
Tuscaloosa, AL

Consultants

Dr. Bonnie Buratti
Jet Propulsion Lab
Pasadena, CA

Dr. Shawn Carlson
Society of Amateur Scientists
San Diego, CA

Dr. Karen Kwitter
Williams College
Williamstown, MA

Dr. Steven Souza
Williamstown, MA

Dr. Joseph P. Straley
University of Kentucky
Lexington, KY

Dr. Thomas Troland
University of Kentucky
Lexington, KY

Dr. Josephine Davis Wallace
University of North Carolina
Charlotte, NC

Consultant for Primary Grades

Donna Harrell Lubcker
East Texas Baptist University
Marshall, TX

Teacher Reviewers (continued)

Beth Lewis
Wilmington, North Carolina

Cindy Hatchell
Wilmington, North Carolina

Cindy Kahler
Carrboro, North Carolina

Diane Leusky
Chapel Hill, North Carolina

Heather Sutton
Wilmington, North Carolina

Crystal Stephens
Valdese, North Carolina

Meg Millard
Chapel Hill, North Carolina

Patricia Underwood
Randleman, North Carolina

E. Joy Mermin
Chapel Hill, North Carolina

Yolanda Evans
Wilmington, North Carolina

Tim Gilbride
Pennsauken, New Jersey

Helene Reifowitz
Nesconset, New York

Tina Craig
Tulsa, Oklahoma

Deborah Harwell
Lawton, Oklahoma

Kathleen Conn
West Chester, Pennsylvania

Heath Renninger Zerbe
Tremont, Pennsylvania

Patricia Armillei
Holland, Pennsylvania

Sue Workman
Cedar City, Utah

Peg Jensen
Hartford, Wisconsin

UNIT B

Life Science

Living Things and Their Environments PAGE B1

For Your Reference

Activities

Unit B

UNIT B

Living Things and Their Environments

LOOK!

A tiny leaf-cutter ant carries off a leaf that is much larger than itself. How do leaf-cutter ants interact with other living things in the rain forest?

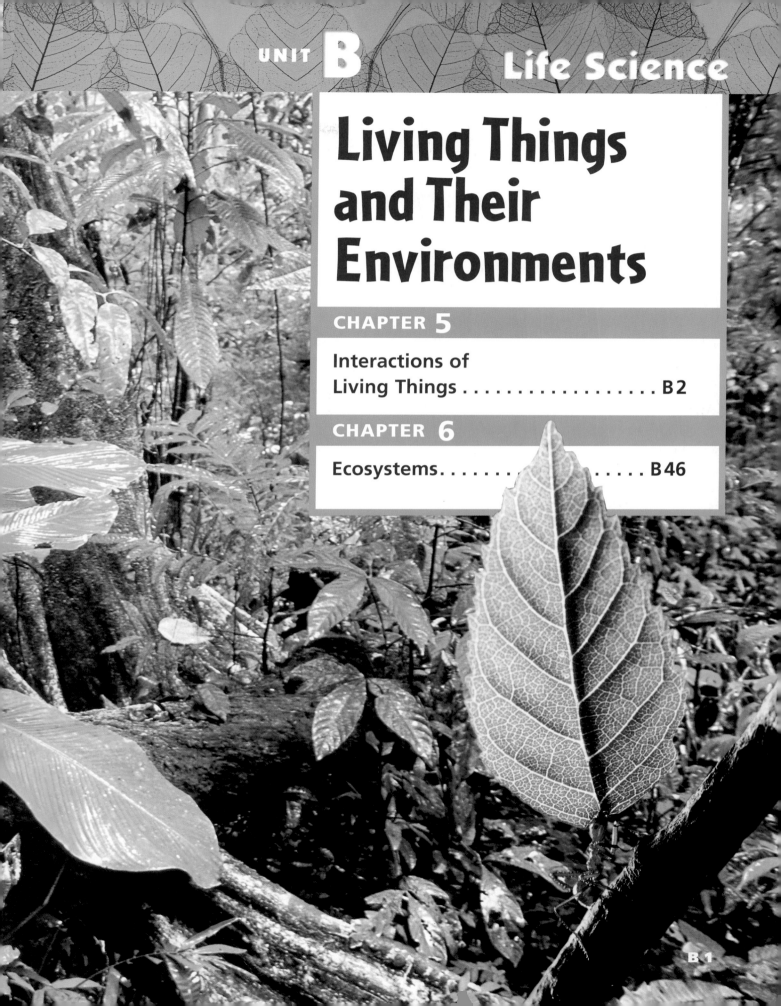

Living Things and Their Environments

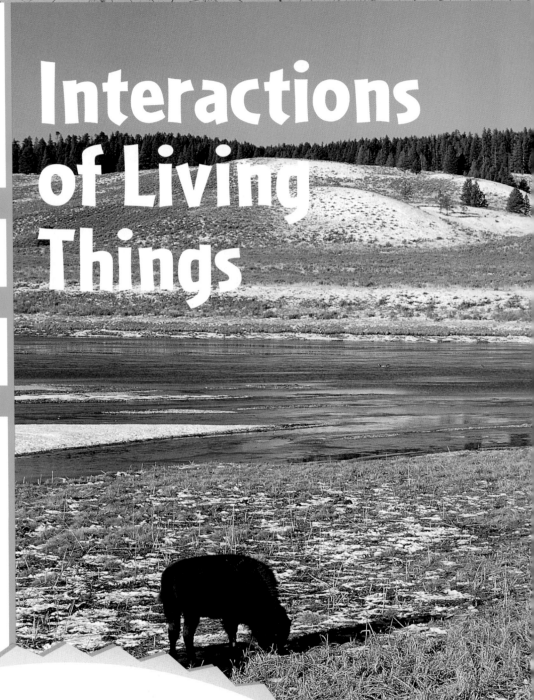

Interactions of Living Things

Did You Ever Wonder?

What happened to the buffalo? The huge herds of buffalo
that once roamed the grasslands of the United States were
hunted almost to extinction. Today, however, buffalo can once
again be seen in places like Yellowstone National Park.

INQUIRY SKILL **Infer** What living and nonliving things affect the life
of the buffalo?

B 3

Interactions in an Ecosystem

Vocabulary

ecosystem, B6
abiotic factor, B6
biotic factor, B7
population, B11
community, B11
ecology, B11
habitat, B12
niche, B12

Get Ready

What do you need in order to survive? Food? Water? Comfortable temperatures? Shelter?

What kinds of things does the animal shown here need to survive? What kinds of things do the plants need? Where do you think they get these things?

Inquiry Skill

You experiment when you perform a test to support or disprove a hypothesis.

Explore Activity

What Do Living Things Need to Survive?

Procedure: Design Your Own

BE CAREFUL! Handle animals and plants gently.

1. For a water environment, add thoroughly washed sand or gravel to the jar. Fill the jar with water. Add a few floating plants, rooted plants with floating leaves, and submerged plants. Add water snails.

2. For a land environment, place a layer of gravel on the bottom of the jar. Cover the gravel layer with a layer of moistened soil. Add plants, and plant grass seeds. Add earthworms, sow bugs, and snails.

3. Place each jar in a lighted area but not in direct sunlight.

4. Cover each jar with its own lid or with a piece of plastic wrap. Record the number and types of living things you used.

5. **Observe** Examine your jars every other day, and record your observations.

Drawing Conclusions

1. **Infer** What are the nonliving parts of your system? What are the living parts of your system?

2. **Infer** What do the living things need to survive? How do you know?

3. **FURTHER INQUIRY** **Experiment** How could you design an environment that contains land and water areas?

Materials

wide-mouthed, clear container with lid

washed gravel

pond water or aged tap water

water plants

water snails

soil

small rocks

grass seed and small plants

earthworms, land snails, sow bugs, or other small land animals that eat plants

What Is an Ecosystem?

What or whom do you interact with every day? Living things and nonliving things interact in an **ecosystem**. An ecosystem is all the living and nonliving things in an area.

An ecosystem may be very small, such as a backyard or pond. Some ecosystems, like the prairie ecosystem of North America, the deserts of Africa, and the rain forests of Brazil, cover large areas of a country or continent. Freshwater ecosystems cover less space than saltwater ecosystems. Saltwater ecosystems can cover entire oceans. It doesn't matter where they are or what they look like, all ecosystems have the same parts.

Abiotic Factors

The nonliving parts of an ecosystem are the **abiotic** (ay·bigh·AHT·ik) **factors**. All living things need certain nonliving things in order to survive. Abiotic factors include water, minerals, sunlight, air, climate, and soil.

All organisms, or living things, need water. Their bodies are 50 to 95 percent water. The processes that keep living things alive—like photosynthesis and respiration—can only take place in the presence of water. Living things also need minerals, such as calcium, iron, phosphorus, and nitrogen. Some living things, like plants and algae, need sunlight to make food. Animals need oxygen to produce energy for their bodies. Plants and algae need carbon dioxide. The environment must also have the right temperature for organisms to survive.

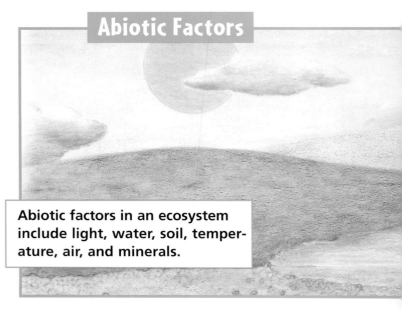

Abiotic Factors

Abiotic factors in an ecosystem include light, water, soil, temperature, air, and minerals.

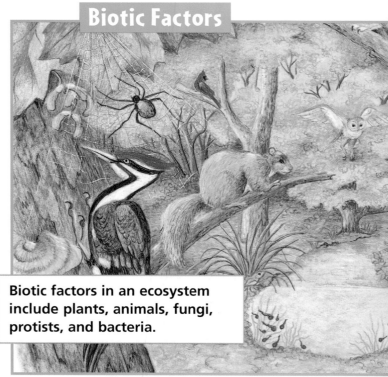

Biotic Factors

Biotic factors in an ecosystem include plants, animals, fungi, protists, and bacteria.

READING
Diagrams

1. How do these two diagrams differ? What does each diagram show?

2. Which of these two diagrams best shows the abiotic factors in the ecosystem? Explain your answer.

Biotic Factors

The living parts of an ecosystem are animals, plants, fungi, protists, and bacteria. These organisms make up the **biotic** (bigh·AHT·ik) **factors** of an ecosystem.

Plants and algae are *producers*. They produce oxygen and food that animals need. Animals are *consumers*. Animals consume, or eat, algae, plants, or animals. Animals also give off carbon dioxide that plants and algae need to make food.

What do the fungi and bacteria contribute? They are a very important part of any ecosystem. Fungi and bacteria are *decomposers*. They *decompose*, or break down, dead plants and animals into useful things like minerals that enrich soil. Plants need these in order to grow. Each kind of organism has a role that helps the others survive.

There are many ecosystems in the world and each has a unique set of biotic and abiotic factors. These factors determine the kinds of organisms that the ecosystem can support. This is why there are different organisms in different ecosystems. For example, you wouldn't find a buffalo in a desert or a forest ecosystem because it needs grass to survive.

▶ **What are five abiotic and five biotic factors in an ecosystem?**

What Is a Prairie Ecosystem Like?

Long ago a "sea of wild grasses" covered North America from central Texas in the south to North Dakota in the north. These were America's prairie lands, the range of the famous song "Home on the Range."

The Blackland Prairie is the largest remaining prairie in America. It stretches 483 km (300 mi) across Texas, from Austin to Clarksville. The Blacklands got their name from the rich black soil the early settlers found there. The settlers found that the summers were hot and long, and that there was enough rain to grow profitable crops, like cotton.

Before the land became farms and ranches, huge herds of buffalo grazed on the prairie grasses. Native Americans once hunted the buffalo on this land for food and clothing as a means of survival.

Buffalo were not the prairie's only inhabitants. Plants and animals of all kinds lived there. At least 50 different kinds of tall and short grasses provided food for plant-eating animals. Many kinds of wildflowers painted the landscape with beautiful colors. These flowers included purple coneflowers, bluebells, yellow sunflowers, and golden daleas. Travelers might have come across oak, hickory, elm, or cedar trees along nearby streams.

The cattle and crops that provide much of our food live on the prairie today. Ranchers and farmers now graze cattle and plant crops such as corn and wheat on the Blacklands.

READING

Sequence of Events
How has the Blackland Prairie ecosystem changed over time?

What Is the Treasure of the Blackland Prairie?

Have you ever read about a buried treasure? Unlike those stories, the treasure of the Blackland Prairie is not buried underground. The treasure of the Blackland Prairie *is* the ground.

Prairie soils can often be identified by their dark brown to black *topsoil*. Topsoil is the top layer of soil. The dark color shows the presence of *humus*. Humus is partly decayed plant matter. The decay is produced by the bacteria and fungi.

The rich topsoil is full of minerals that prairie grasses and crops need. Two of the most important minerals are magnesium and calcium. Plants need magnesium in order to make chlorophyll. Calcium is an important element of cell walls in plants.

The Blackland Prairie covers almost 13 million acres. Many kinds of animals and plants live on a prairie. A prairie is a region of grasses. It may be flat or hilly grassland.

The nutrients in certain prairie soils tend to stay near the surface. That's true because of the low yearly rainfall on prairies. There isn't enough water to carry the nutrients deep into the ground. Farmers take advantage of this by growing crops that have shallow roots, such as corn, wheat, cotton, and sorghum. Sorghum is a grain that is used to feed livestock. What do these crops have in common with the plants that grow naturally on the prairie? They are all classified as grasses.

▷ **How can you describe the soil of the Blackland Prairie?**

Prairie dogs

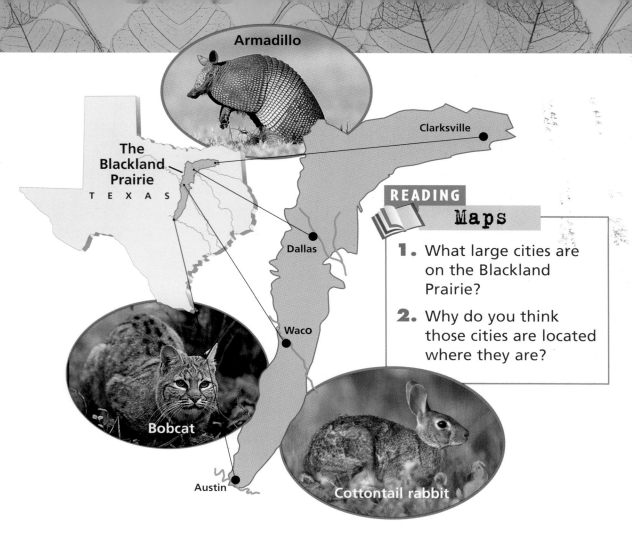

Armadillo

The Blackland Prairie
T E X A S

Clarksville

Dallas

Waco

Austin

Bobcat

Cottontail rabbit

READING
Maps

1. What large cities are on the Blackland Prairie?

2. Why do you think those cities are located where they are?

What Animals Live on the Blackland Prairie?

About 500 species, or different kinds, of animals still live on this prairie. The spotted chorus frog sings in the night near the streams and rivers. Rattlesnakes and lizards seek shelter under rocks.

Birds like pipits, longspurs, and horned larks, as well as 300 other kinds of birds, still live on the Blackland Prairie.

Raccoons, opossums, coyotes, white-tailed deer, and striped skunks live on the Blacklands. Cotton rats, white-footed mice, eastern cottontails, red bats, and bobcats live there, too.

Mountain lions, gray wolves, black bears, and jaguars used to come in search of prey. When people came and built towns, cities, and farms, the buffalo left. The animals that fed on the buffalo left, too. Some animals, however, came to the Blacklands from other places, and stayed. Armadillos arrived from Mexico as the Blacklands' climate warmed up over the past 150 years. Badgers invaded from north-western Texas when their natural homes were cleared for development.

▷ **What are five animals that live on the prairie?**

What Are Populations and Communities?

The Blackland Prairie, like all ecosystems, is home to many different organisms. Each kind of organism, whether an animal, plant, fungus, protist, or bacterium, is a member of a different species. All the organisms of a species living in the same area make up a **population**.

The Blackland Prairie has populations of armadillos and badgers. It has populations of little bluestem grass and Indian grass. It has elm trees. It also has populations of pond algae and soil bacteria. All the populations living in an area make up a **community**.

The populations in a community interact with each other in different ways. Scientists who are interested in these interactions are ecologists.

Ecology is the study of how all things in an ecosystem interact.

Ecologists investigate the activities of animals, plants, fungi, protists, and bacteria in the ecosystem. They want to know which animals prey on others. Which animals eat plants? Which insects eat crops? They are interested in how bacteria and fungi make the soil fertile. All these questions need to be answered to understand how an ecosystem stays healthy.

▷ **What are populations and communities?**

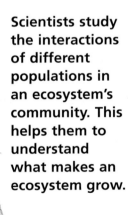

Scientists study the interactions of different populations in an ecosystem's community. This helps them to understand what makes an ecosystem grow.

What Are Niches and Habitats?

The place where an organism lives is called its **habitat**. The chorus frog's habitat is in the scattered ponds of the Blacklands.

Each species in an ecosystem also has a role or place in the activities of its community. The role of an organism in the community is its **niche**.

A species' niche includes many factors. It includes what a species eats and what eats that species. It includes the kind of environment the species needs to live in. It even includes whether the species is active by day or night.

No two populations can have the same niche. Why is this true? To have the same niche, two populations would have to eat the same foods and be eaten by the same predators. They would have to live in the same space and reproduce in the same ways. They would have to grow under the same temperature, moisture, and light conditions, get the same diseases, and look and behave exactly alike. They would have to be identical! No two populations are identical though, so no two populations have the same niche.

Scientists study the habitats and niches of organisms in a community. They do this to see if the community is healthy or in trouble.

The red bat's habitat is above the ground. During the day it hangs from tree branches like a red leaf. At night it streaks through the air looking for food.

▶ **What is the difference between a niche and a habitat?**

The horned lark has its niche on the prairie.

How Do Organisms Change Their Environment?

You have learned how plants and animals adapt to their environment. However, living organisms also change the environment where they live. These changes can be good, neutral, or bad for the ecosystem.

Have you ever seen a beaver pond? Beavers cut down trees by gnawing their way through tree trunks. Then, they use the tree trunks to build dams that back up water into ponds. Beaver ponds filter sediment and organic matter that otherwise would be carried downstream. The filtered organic matter provides nutrients for invertebrates and aquatic plants.

These invertebrates and aquatic plants attract breeding waterfowl and many fish species. Soon fish-eating animals such as otters follow.

Beaver ponds eventually become marshy areas which allow certain trees to grow. Over time, the marshy area becomes a meadow, and later shrubs begin to grow. The shrubs provide shade that allows tree seedlings to get started. The trees eventually grow into a mature forest.

▷ **How do beavers change their environment?**

QUICK LAB

Changing the Environment

FOLDABLES™ Make a Shutter Fold. (See p. R 42.) Label the shutters as shown.

Changes to the Environment | Things Affected by Changes

1. Select a wild animal that you find interesting. It can be as small as an insect or as large as whale.

2. Do research to find where this animal lives and what it does to survive in its environment.

3. Draw or find a picture of the animal you selected and paste it in the center of the Shutter Fold.

4. **Communicate** How does the animal you selected change the environment where it lives? What living things are affected by these changes? Write your answers on the Shutter Fold.

5. **Infer** How do the living things you listed above adapt to the changes in their environment? Write your answer on the back of your Shutter Fold.

How Do Organisms Survive in Variable Environments?

The world is a place of changes. As you read on the previous page, some of these changes are caused by living organisms. Some other changes are weather related.

One day the weather may be dry and cold. The next day it may be wet and warm. Heavy rains may drench the land one spring and summer. The next year's spring and summer may have cloudless skies day after day. This makes habitats change.

A good habitat for a certain organism at one time may be a threatening one at another time. How do organisms survive difficult times?

Organisms find new habitats or adapt to the changes in their habitat.

The Eastern Spadefoot Toad

The eastern spadefoot toad lives on the Blackland Prairie. This animal reproduces in water and needs water for its daily life. What happens if a drought strikes the Blacklands?

A close look at the toad's hind feet provided scientists with a clue to the answer. Its hind feet are shaped like little spades. They are adapted for digging. That's just what the spadefoot toad does when water is scarce. It digs into the ground and covers itself with soil. This toad can absorb water through its skin. There's a lot of clay in Blacklands soil, and clay holds water well. Usually there is some water in the soil, even though there may not be any water above it. The toad may be able to survive in the soil even during a drought.

▷ **What happens to animals when habitats change?**

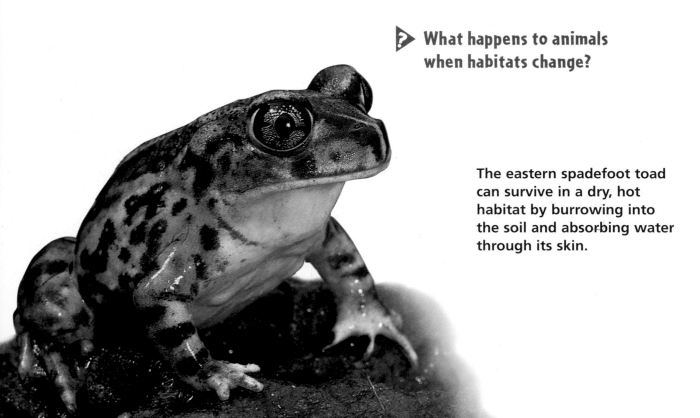

The eastern spadefoot toad can survive in a dry, hot habitat by burrowing into the soil and absorbing water through its skin.

Why It Matters

Ecosystems in nature tend to stay in balance. This balance, however, can be upset by the actions of people. Cities are built on the land. Crops are cultivated. The land changes. Its natural inhabitants disappear. People gain certain things but lose others. It is important to make wise decisions when you think of changing an ecosystem. Otherwise you may lose more than you gain.

 e-Journal Visit our Web site **www.science.mmhschool.com** to do a research project on an ecosystem of your choice.

Think and Write

1. Describe the structure of an ecosystem.

2. What is the difference between a population and a community?

3. How does an animal's habitat relate to its niche?

4. How do light, temperature, and soil composition affect an ecosystem's capacity to support life?

5. **Critical Thinking** Identify changes caused by human activity in your ecosystem. Explain what was lost and what was gained. Evaluate the results.

L·I·N·K·S

ART LINK

Make a poster. Visit a local ecosystem like a park, pond, or even your backyard. Draw all the living and nonliving things you see. Discuss the similarities and differences between the communities and interactions of the ecosystem you visited, and an ecosystem you studied in class.

WRITING LINK

Writing That Compares Research the biotic and abiotic factors of the Blackland Prairie and the Everglades in Florida. Compare these two ecosystems. Tell how the ecosystems are similar. Then write about their differences.

MATH LINK

Problem solving. A group of ecologists has counted 7,522 American Robins, 12,788 Northern Cardinals, and 3,657 Ruby-throated Hummingbirds in the Piedmont area. Order birds from the least number to the greatest.

TECHNOLOGY LINK

LOG ON Visit **www.science.mmhschool.com** for more links.

Interactions Among Living Things

Vocabulary

food chain, B18
food web, B20
herbivore, B20
carnivore, B20
predator, B21
prey, B21
scavenger, B21
omnivore, B21
symbiosis, B24
mutualism, B25
parasitism, B26
commensalism, B27

Get Ready

Populations provide energy-rich food for one another. Grasses and other green plants provide food for gazelles. Lions feed on gazelles. What do you think might happen if a drought reduced the number of grasses? How can changes in a population lead to changes in the ecosystem where it lives?

Inquiry Skill

You predict when you state possible results of an event or experiment.

Explore Activity

How Do Populations Interact?

Materials

tape

string

population cards

Procedure

1. Cut out the cards representing the plants and animals in the ecosystem.

2. Label the top of your paper *Sunlight*.

3. Place the plant cards on the paper, and link each to the sunlight with tape and string.

4. Link each plant-eating animal to a plant card. Link each meat-eating animal to its food source. Only two animals can be attached to a food source. Record the links you have made.

5. Fire destroys half the plants. Remove four plant cards. Rearrange the animal cards. Remove animal cards if more than two animals link to any one food source. Record the changes you have made.

Drawing Conclusions

1. **Observe** What has happened to the plant eaters as a result of the fire? To the animal eaters?

2. **Infer** Half of the plants that were lost in the fire grow back again. What happens to the animal populations?

3. **Experiment** Try adding or removing plant or animal cards. What happens to the rest of the populations?

4. FURTHER INQUIRY **Predict** If plants or prey become scarce, their predators may move to a new area. What will happen to the ecosystem the predators move into?

Grasshopper
Food: prairie plants

Meadowlark
Food: crickets, grasshoppers

Ground Squirrel
Food: prairie plants

Bullsnake
Food: mice, rabbits, ground squirrels, birds and eggs.

Red-Tailed Hawk
Food: ground squirrels, mice, rabbits, snakes, lizards, small birds

Prairie Plants
Food: made from water, carbon dioxide, and sunlight

Coyote
Food: rabbits, ground squirrels, meadow mice, other rodents

Main Idea Food chains and food webs describe the feeding relationship in an ecosystem.

What Is a Food Chain?

How important is a small change in a population? Changes in one population can affect several other populations in the same ecosystem. Every population needs energy in order to survive. Where does that energy come from? The energy in an ecosystem comes from the Sun.

You can feel the Sun's energy as it warms your skin. A meadow mouse scurrying through a Blacklands cornfield and a red-tailed hawk diving to snare the mouse can feel it, too. Neither of these animals can directly use the Sun's energy. However, they must have it to move, to breathe, to keep their hearts beating, and to stay alive.

The energy of the Sun is stored in food. The energy in food is passed from one organism to another in a **food chain**. A food chain is the path energy takes from producers to consumers to decomposers.

On the prairie the first organisms in a food chain are plants. Plants capture the Sun's energy during photosynthesis. This energy is stored in foods, or sugars, the plant makes for itself.

What happens when a plant eater such as a grasshopper eats the plant? Animals use the oxygen they breathe to release energy from the energy-rich sugars they eat. Some of the energy is released for the grasshopper to use. Some of the energy is also stored in its tissues. Some is lost as heat. A Texas horned lizard may snap up the grasshopper, and a red-tailed hawk may eat the lizard. In the prairie

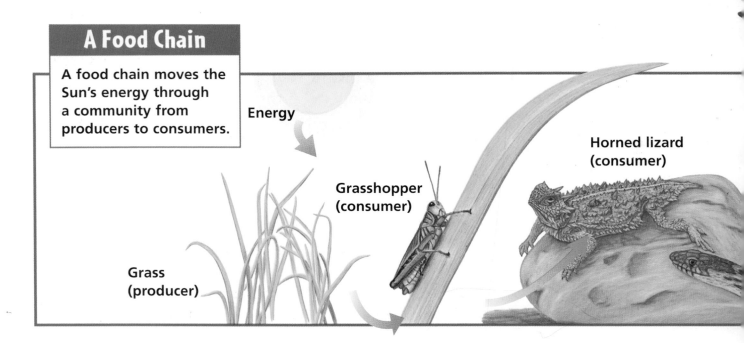

A Food Chain

A food chain moves the Sun's energy through a community from producers to consumers.

Energy

Grasshopper (consumer)

Horned lizard (consumer)

Grass (producer)

community, the hawk is one of the organisms at the top of the food chain. It eats snakes, mice, lizards, rabbits, and other birds.

The red-tailed hawk doesn't eat plants. However, because of the food chain, it gets some of the Sun's energy that was originally stored in plants.

Plants and animals become food for small organisms like crickets and ants when they die. They are also a food source for microscopic organisms like bacteria.

▷ **What does a food chain show?**

READING
Diagrams

1. What are the members of this food chain?

2. Where does the food chain begin? End?

Red-tailed hawk (consumer)

Soil bacteria (decomposers)

QUICK LAB

Getting Food

FOLDABLES™ Make a Shutter Fold. (See p. R 42.) Label the shutters as shown.

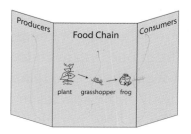

Producers · Food Chain · Consumers

plant → grasshopper → frog

1. Take a walk outdoors around your home or school. Choose a community to study. Make a list of the living things you see. Don't include people or domestic animals like dogs, cats, and farm animals. You may want to take photos to complete your observations.

2. **Classify** Divide the organisms into two groups in your Shutter Fold—those that can make their own food (producers) on the left and those that cannot (consumers) on the right.

3. **Classify** Which organisms did you list as producers?

4. **Classify** Which organisms did you list as consumers?

5. **Communicate** Draw one or more food chains in your Shutter Fold to show how energy moves through this community.

What Is a Food Web?

Do all organisms eat only one food? Are all organisms eaten by only one type of animal? No. Animals often eat or are eaten by many different things. How can we study all of the things that an animal eats or is eaten by? A food chain only shows the path of energy as it moves from one organism to another. A **food web** shows the relationship between all of the species in a community. It shows how populations must compete for food. A food web is a map of overlapping food chains.

Producers

All food webs begin with *producers*. The producers on land include grasses, trees, and all other organisms that use the Sun's energy to make their own food. In oceans the main producers are algae.

Plant Eaters

Organisms that cannot make their own food are *consumers*. Consumers get energy from the food made by other organisms. Consumers can be grouped according to the type of food they eat. **Herbivores**

(HUR·buh·vawrz) eat producers. Both Earth's land and waters are filled with herbivores—animals that eat plants, algae, and other producers.

Meat Eaters

Herbivores, in turn, are eaten by **carnivores** (KAHR·nuh·vawrz)—animals that eat other animals. All cats, big and small, are carnivores. So are dogs, wolves, foxes, coyotes, and other sharp-toothed animals. The sea also has carnivores. One of the largest of these is the great white shark.

Land Food Web

Snakes · Hawks · Mountain lions · Insect-eating birds · Seed-eating birds · Deer · Rabbits · Mice · Bark beetles · Grass · Grasshoppers · Seeds · Trees · Fungi · Earthworms

READING Diagrams

Which of these animals are predators? Which of these animals are prey?

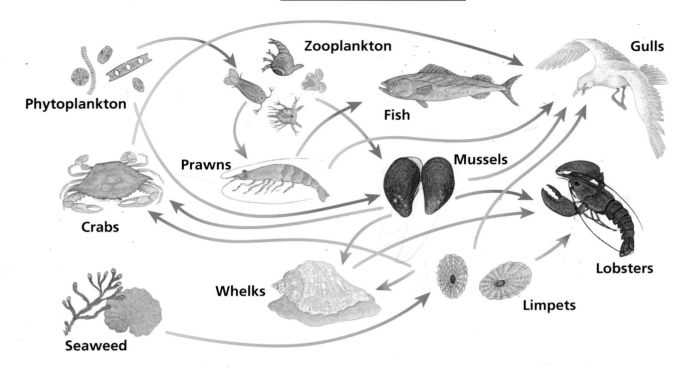

Phytoplankton · Zooplankton · Gulls · Fish · Prawns · Mussels · Crabs · Lobsters · Whelks · Limpets · Seaweed

Other sea dwellers also eat meat. Seals, dolphins, and whales dine on fish, squid, and even penguins.

Living things that hunt other living things for food are **predators**. The hunted are called **prey**. The relationships between predators and prey are a key part of both food chains and food webs.

However, not all meat eaters are predators. Some animals eat meat but don't hunt it. Such meat eaters are called **scavengers**. They feed on the remains of dead animals. Have you ever seen vultures circling a spot of land? Then you have seen scavengers. Crows are also scavengers. You might see them on a road, pecking at the body of an animal.

The sea is home to many scavengers. One of these is the hagfish. It wanders the ocean floor in search of dead or dying fish. Some tiny sea creatures also feed on the remains of dead sea animals.

When an animal eats both animals and plants, it is an **omnivore**. You are an omnivore. Bears are omnivores, too, eating things from berries to salmon.

Decomposers

Every food chain and food web ends with *decomposers* such as worms, insects, bacteria, and fungi. These organisms break down dead matter into substances that can be used by producers. Decomposers break down dead organisms and wastes into simpler substances. Some of these substances are absorbed by the decomposers. Some are returned to the soil.

▷ **What are the parts of a food web?**

How Are Populations Connected?

What would happen if farmers used powerful insecticides to kill pests? What might happen if these pesticides also killed some harmless ants? Ants live in the same habitat as Texas horned lizards. Because the lizards eat ants, changes in the ant population may tell a lot about the future of the lizards.

In the food chain, the relationship doesn't stop there. Birds of prey, such as hawks, feed on the lizards. What happens to the ants will also affect the lives of these birds. A change in one population affects all the other organisms in that food chain.

Animals may adapt to changes in their habitats. A varied diet can be useful. Texas horned lizards eat mainly ants. They also eat other insects such as grasshoppers. If the ant population decreases, the lizards can feed on grasshoppers instead. This changes the number of grasshoppers in a community, however. The other organisms that eat grasshoppers will be affected, too. A change in the ant population affects more than just a food chain. It affects all of the organisms in a food web.

Food chains and food webs help scientists predict how communities will be affected by change.

Lubber grasshoppers

Ant

READING **Sequence of Events**
How does a change in a food web affect other populations?

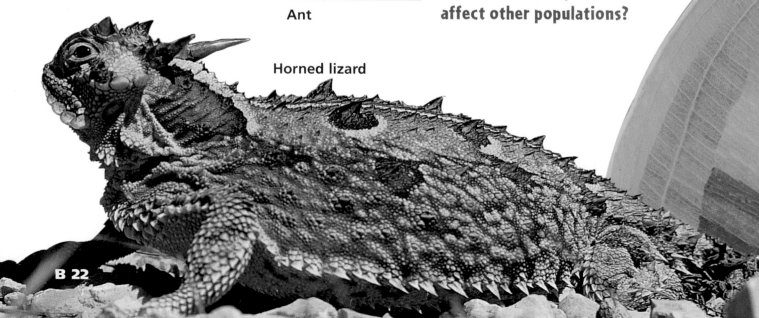

Horned lizard

How Do Populations Adapt to Competition for Food?

Food webs show that animals compete for food. Fish and gulls must compete for a dinner of prawns, for example. In order to survive, an organism must adapt to competition. Sometimes this competition causes a population to change its habitat. This is what happened to Florida's green anole.

At one time green anoles could be spotted all over Florida, perched on the trunks of trees and the branches of bushes. Then a new and bigger species of anole arrived in Florida from the island of Cuba. Scientists don't know how it made the 144 km (90 mi) trip. Its size and, perhaps, other characteristics gave it a hunting edge over the small green anole, however.

Soon the smaller green anole seemed to disappear. Was it really gone? No. Scientists found the little green anole high in the trees. It had found a new habitat where it did not have to compete with the Cuban anole for food.

▷ **How did the green anole adapt to competition?**

The green anole (left), a native of the U.S. southeast, acquired a new habitat when Cuban anoles (above) were introduced.

What Is Symbiosis?

Organisms interact with each other in a number of different ways. You have already seen that some organisms hunt others. Some organisms are predators. Some organisms are prey. You have also seen that organisms may compete with each other for food or territory. Two different kinds of predators may hunt the same prey. However, there are also other kinds of relationships between different kinds of organisms. Some of these relationships are long lasting.

In nature a relationship between two kinds of organisms that lasts over a period of time is called **symbiosis**. There are different kinds of symbiosis. Sometimes both organisms benefit from the relationship. Sometimes one organism benefits while harming the other. Sometimes only one benefits, and the other is not affected. Let's take a closer look at each kind of symbiosis.

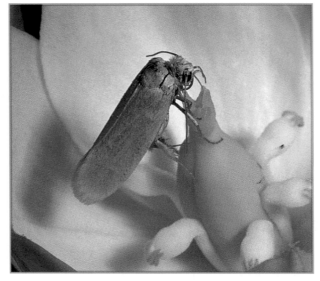

Yucca moth

> **What is symbiosis?**

Mojave Desert

READING

Maps

Describe where in the United States the Mojave Desert is.

What Is Mutualism?

When a relationship between two kinds of organisms benefits both of them, it is called **mutualism**.

A strange-looking plant grows in the Mojave Desert of southern California. It's called a Joshua tree, or yucca plant.

When this tree's creamy flowers are in bloom, small gray shadows seem to dart from flower to flower. A more careful look reveals that the "shadows" are actually moths. These are yucca moths.

Yucca trees and yucca moths depend on each other for survival. Each helps the other reproduce.

The Yucca Moth and the Yucca Tree

Yucca moths cannot survive without yucca trees. The yucca trees would also quickly become extinct if the moths vanished. The yucca moths and the yucca trees benefit from each other and share a relationship of mutualism. How does this work?

At night a female yucca moth visits a yucca flower. Inside the flower the moth picks up pollen and rolls it up into a ball, which it holds gently in its mouth. Then the moth flutters over to another flower. There it makes a hole in the flower's ovary. The moth injects its eggs through the hole. Finally, it packs the sticky ball of pollen onto the flower's stigma. The stigma and ovary are female reproductive parts of a flower. Pollen holds male sex cells.

In protecting its eggs, the moth has also pollinated the yucca flower. The pollinated flower can then make seeds. Eventually some of the seeds will sprout into new yucca plants. This means yucca plants will continue to grow in the desert.

The moth's eggs and the tree's seeds develop at the same time. When the eggs hatch into larvae, the larvae will feed on some of the seeds. All this is happening inside the protective ovary wall. The larvae are not only getting needed food, they are also safe from predators.

▷ **How is mutualism an example of symbiosis?**

What Is Parasitism?

A relationship in which one kind of organism lives on or in another organism and may harm that organism is called **parasitism** (PAR·uh·sigh·tiz·uhm). The organisms that live on or in other organisms are called *parasites* (PAR·uh·sights). The organisms they feed on are called *hosts*. The parasites benefit from the relationship. The hosts are harmed by it.

Fleas are parasites of dogs and cats. The fleas live off the blood of these hosts and give nothing back but itching and irritation. Plants also have parasites, which often are other plants.

The bright orange dodder plant has little chlorophyll. This means that it can't make enough food to live on. Instead it winds around a plant that can make its own food. The dodder then sends tubes into the stem of the plant it is coiled around. Next, the dodder gets food from the plant through the tubes. Although the plant it lives on usually does not die, it is weakened, grows more slowly, and is not able to easily fight off diseases.

▷ **How does parasitism differ from mutualism?**

The coiling dodder plant, which can't make enough of its own food, draws food from other plants.

Mistletoe is another parasitic plant. It is an evergreen that grows on the trunk or branches of trees such as hawthorn, poplar, fir, or apple.

Flea

The remora picks up the scraps that the loggerhead sea turtle discards.

Orchids benefit from their position on the trunks of trees.

What Is Commensalism?

Few plants can grow on the floor of a rain forest. The thick canopy above keeps light from reaching the ground. Some plants, like orchids, attach themselves to the trunks of trees high above the rain forest floor. The orchids don't take anything from the trees. They simply use the trees to get needed sunlight. This relationship, in which one organism benefits from another without harming or helping it, is called **commensalism** (kuh·MEN·suh·liz·uhm).

Many animals also have this kind of relationship. The remora's dorsal fin is modified into a sucker with which it forms a temporary attachment to the loggerhead sea turtle. When the turtle feeds, the remora picks up scraps. The turtle provides food to the remora. However, the remora neither harms nor helps the loggerhead sea turtle.

▷ **What kind of relationship is commensalism?**

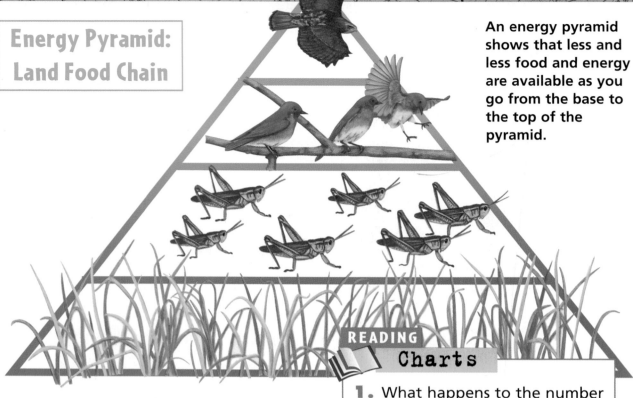

Energy Pyramid: Land Food Chain

An energy pyramid shows that less and less food and energy are available as you go from the base to the top of the pyramid.

How Does Energy Move in a Community?

Plants capture energy from sunlight. When you eat a plant, how much of that energy do you get? All organisms need energy to live. Producers get energy from the Sun. Consumers get it from the foods they eat. However, energy is lost as it passes from one organism to another in a food chain.

You can see the effect of this in the drawing of the energy pyramid on this page. An energy pyramid shows a number of things. It shows that there is less food at the top of the pyramid than at the base. It also shows that there are fewer organisms as you move from bottom to top.

Consumers get their energy from food. The less food there is, the less

READING

Charts

1. What happens to the number of organisms at each level of the pyramid starting from the base?

2. How much more energy from the Sun was available to the grass than to the bluebirds?

energy is available. Energy decreases from the base to the top of the pyramid.

In an ocean community in the Antarctic, algae form the base. Algae are producers that store energy from the Sun. Small fish that live in the icy waters eat some of these algae. The algae that are not eaten are lost to the community. Their energy is not passed up to the next level of the pyramid. Only some of the energy the fish get is passed up to the next level. The fish use some of the energy in swimming and other activities.

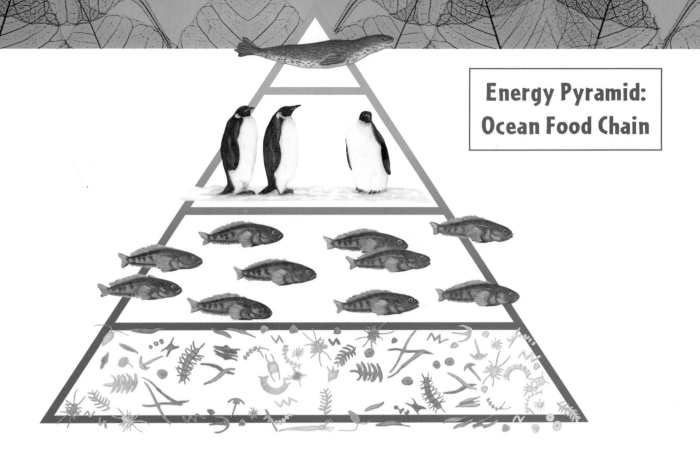

Energy Pyramid: Ocean Food Chain

The penguins dive for the small fish and eat as many as they can catch. Many fish get away. Nevertheless, the penguins have snared some energy-rich fish as food. Some of the energy from the fish is stored in the penguins' tissues. Some of the energy is used to heat their bodies. A dip in the frigid water removes some of this heat from the penguins' bodies. Now they have less energy than they took in from the fish.

Rising from below, a leopard seal clamps its sharp teeth around a helpless penguin and eats it. Does this predator get all the energy that was originally in the algae the fish ate? No. Energy has been lost at each level in the pyramid.

Kilogram for kilogram there are fewer fish than algae. There are fewer penguins than fish. There are fewer leopard seals than penguins. That's because there is less food and energy available at each higher level in the energy pyramid. The less food and energy there are, the fewer living things that can be supported.

How much energy is lost from one level of an energy pyramid to the next? Scientists have actually measured it. The startling figure is 90 percent! Of all the Sun's energy captured by the algae, the leopard seal gets only one-tenth of one percent.

▶ **What does an energy pyramid show?**

How Do Food Webs Affect You?

"Red Tide Observed off the Coast of Maine" might not seem like a scary headline. You might even ignore this important warning. However, it could mean trouble for the average person.

On page B28 you learned that single-celled organisms called algae are at the base of the marine food web. When the algae population increases very rapidly, or blooms, it can turn hundreds of square miles of ocean red. Scientists call this a red tide. Most red tides are not harmful. However, some algae produce poisons. Fire algae are an example. A bloom of these algae is very dangerous to all the species in a food web.

Small fish and mussels feed on the algae. The algae's poison may kill or infect the fish. The decline in the fish population reduces the energy available to the consumers that feed on fish.

How does this affect you? People who eat contaminated fish may become very sick. You are part of a food web, too. Humans are at the top of most food webs. Changes in any population may also affect you.

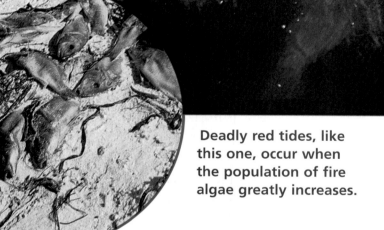

Deadly red tides, like this one, occur when the population of fire algae greatly increases.

▶ How can changes in a food web affect you?

Why It Matters

The lives of all organisms, including humans, are affected by other living things. If the population of one organism in a food chain disappears, the whole food chain is disturbed. If a food chain, food web, or energy pyramid changes, the result will affect humans. By understanding how living things interact with one another people can help preserve the treasures of nature.

e-Journal Visit our Web site www.science.mmhschool.com to do a research project on interactions among living things.

Think and Write

1. What is the original source of energy in an ecosystem?

2. Is it possible to have a food chain that has only a producer and a decomposer?

3. What is the relationship between a food chain and a food web?

4. How is mutualism like commensalism? How is it different?

5. **Critical Thinking** Think about human relationships that are symbiotic. Explain what makes the relationship symbiotic. Who is helped? Who is the helper?

MATH LINK

Use percents. An energy pyramid shows that 90 percent of the energy is lost from one level to the next. If you start with 100,000 units of energy, how much energy does the next level get? The fourth level?

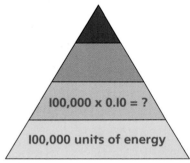

100,000 x 0.10 = ?

100,000 units of energy

WRITING LINK

Writing a Story Stories have a setting, characters, and a sequence of events. They also have a theme, or central idea. Write a story whose theme is a changing ecosystem. Make sure the events in your story involve the lives or activities of your characters.

HEALTH LINK

Investigate parasites. How do parasites affect humans? What do these organisms gain from their host? How do they harm it? Write a paragraph on this topic.

TECHNOLOGY LINK

LOG ON Visit www.science.mmhschool.com for more links.

How Populations Survive

Get Ready

What affects the size of a population? Some forests are so thick with trees and shrubs that you would have a tough time hiking through them. However, hiking through other forests would be as easy as walking down a country road or the street in front of your house. What makes some areas crowded and others empty? What do organisms need in an environment in order to survive?

Inquiry Skill

You communicate when you share information.

Explore Activity

What Controls the Growth of Populations?

Materials

4 small, clean milk cartons with the tops removed

40 pinto bean seeds that have been soaked overnight

soil

water

Procedure

1. Label the cartons 1 to 4. Fill cartons 1 and 2 with dry potting soil. Fill cartons 3 and 4 with moistened potting soil. Fill the cartons to within 2 cm of the top.

2. Plant ten seeds in each carton, and cover the seeds with 0.5 cm of soil.

3. **Use Variables** Place cartons 1 and 3 in a well-lighted area. Place cartons 2 and 4 in a dark place. Label the cartons to show if they are wet or dry and in the light or in the dark.

4. **Observe** Examine the cartons each day for four days. Keep the soil moist in cartons 3 and 4. Record your observations.

5. Observe the plants for two weeks after they sprout. Continue to keep the soil moist in cartons 3 and 4, and record your observations.

Drawing Conclusions

1. **Communicate** How many seeds sprouted in each carton?

2. **Observe** After two weeks how many plants in each carton were still living?

3. Why did some seeds sprout and then die?

4. FURTHER INQUIRY **Infer** Use your observations to explain what is needed for seeds to sprout and what is needed for bean plants to grow. Use evidence to support your explanation.

Main Idea Living and nonliving things interact in ecosystems.

What Controls the Growth of Populations?

How much do living things depend on conditions in their environment in order to survive? Certain factors control the growth and survival of living things. What do these factors include?

A dry wind howls across the prairie. The hot Sun bakes the ground below. No rain has fallen in days. Grasses have withered. Plant-eating insects have gone hungry.

High in the bright, cloudless sky, a hawk flies one way and then another. Its sharp eyes sweep over the barren land below. An unsuspecting deer mouse scurries along the ground in search of an insect.

The mouse's tan fur blends in with the dusty soil, but its movement gives it away. The hawk tucks in its wings and dives like a falling rock. In a flash its talons grab the mouse.

Hidden in this story are clues to how the size of a population is limited. Anything that controls the growth or survival of a population is called a **limiting factor**.

Some limiting factors are nonliving. In the story the sunlight, wind, water, and temperature were nonliving limiting factors. They controlled the population of grasses on the prairie.

The grasses, insects, deer mice, and hawks were living limiting factors. The grasses had withered. There was less food for plant-eating insects, so the number of insects living on the prairie decreased. That meant there was less food for the insect-eating deer mice. The deer mouse population was also limited by the hawks, which are predators.

The number of predators in an ecosystem affects the number of prey. The number of prey in an ecosystem can also determine how many predators the ecosystem can support. If there were few hawks, the deer mouse population

Organisms like coyotes (above) and raccoons (left) compete with each other for resources such as food, water, and territory.

might stay steady or even rise. More hawks, however, mean fewer deer mice.

Hawks compete with other predators, like coyotes and raccoons. Coyotes and raccoons hunt many animals, including small rodents like deer mice. Coyotes and raccoons also compete with each other for food, water, and places to live. The population that wins such competitions is likely to grow.

However, even a growing population faces problems. Its size will soon limit its own growth. The organisms in the population will become crowded. They will have to compete with one another for food, water, and shelter. Some will die. Eventually there will be enough resources for the number of organisms that remain. The maximum population size that the resources in an area can support is called the **carrying capacity**.

READING **Sequence of Events** **Explain how a change in the coyote population could affect the number of mice in an area.**

Overcrowding, as in this group of walruses, limits the growth of any population.

QUICK LAB

Playground Space

FOLDABLES Make a Folded Table. (See p. R 44.) Label it as shown. Record your results in the Folded Table.

	How Much Space?
#3 Use Numbers	
#4 Infer	
#5 Infer	

1. **Measure** Use a meterstick to measure the sides of your playground.

2. Multiply the length by the width to find the area in square meters. If your playground is irregular, use triangles and squares to find the area.

3. **Use Numbers** To find out how much space each student has, divide the area of the playground by the number of students.

4. **Infer** What would happen to the space each student had if the number of students doubled?

5. **Infer** Suppose two other classes with the same number of students as yours used the playground at the same time as your class. What effect might this have on your class?

6. **Compare** your area and space per student with the results that other groups obtained. Are there any discrepancies? Explain.

What Happens When Habitats Are Changed?

Did you know that American bald eagles were once found in almost every part of the United States? When the first European settlers sailed to American shores, bald eagles roamed the skies of the Atlantic and the Pacific coasts. They inhabited every large river and lake in North America.

Bald eagles need wilderness areas with tall trees to nest and perch in, and clean waters to fish in, to survive. However, as the human population settled all over North America, the bald eagle's natural habitat disappeared, and their food supplies decreased. When this happened, eagles started feeding on chickens and other domestic livestock and large numbers were shot by people. By the late 1800s, the population of bald eagles had sharply declined.

In 1940 the Bald Eagle Act was passed. As a result, eagle populations began to recover. At the same time, however, DDT and other pesticides began to be widely used. Pesticides sprayed on plants were eaten by small animals, which were later eaten by birds of prey. The DDT poison harmed both the adult birds and the eggs that they laid. The egg shells became too thin and were often crushed. Eggs that were not crushed during incubation often did not hatch. Large quantities of DDT were discovered in the bodies of adult bald eagles too.

Bald eagles were once common on the Blackland Prairie.

When the effects of DDT were understood, people all over the country worked to help save the bald eagle. DDT was banned and laws continued to protect our national symbol. In 1976, the U. S. Fish and Wildlife Service officially listed the bald eagle as an **endangered species**. This means that a species is in danger of becoming **extinct**. A species is extinct when it has died out completely.

The bald eagle population responded well to these conservation measures. The number of bald eagles went from less than 850 in 1963 to almost 13,000 in 2000 in the lower 48 states. In 1995, the bald eagle's status was upgraded to **threatened species**. This means that the species may become endangered. Today, about half of the world's 70,000 bald eagles live in Alaska.

▷ **Why did bald eagles start feeding on domestic livestock?**

Inquiry Skill BUILDER

Vanishing Bald Eagles

The table below shows the average number of bald eagle eggs that hatched in the wild during a 16-year period. It also shows the level of an insecticide in bald eagle eggs during the same period. What is the relationship between these two variables?

Variables are things that can change. In order to determine what caused the results of an experiment, you need to change one variable at a time. The variable that is changed is called the *independent variable*. A *dependent variable* is one that changes because of the independent variable.

Materials

ruler

Bald Eagle Egg-Hatching Data																
Year	1966	1967	1968	1969	1970	1971	1972*	1973	1974	1975	1976	1977	1978	1979	1980	1981
Average number of young hatched (per nest)	1.28	0.75	0.87	0.82	0.50	0.55	0.60	0.70	0.60	0.81	0.90	0.93	0.91	0.98	1.02	1.27
Insecticide in eggs (parts per million)	42	68	125	119	122	108	82	74	68	59	32	12	13	14	13	13

*pesticide banned

Procedure

1 **Infer** What is the independent variable in the study? What is the dependent variable in the study?

2 **Communicate** Make a line graph showing the average number of young that hatched. Make another line graph showing the amount of insecticide in eggs.

Drawing Conclusions

1 **Use Variables** Based on the graphs, what appears to be the relationship between the amount of insecticide in eggs and the number of young hatched?

2 **Hypothesize** Suggest a reason for the relationship.

How Do People Change the Environment?

The two competitors face off. There is an enormous silence in the tenseness of the moment. Slowly, silently, heads and shoulders are lowered. Then they charge and their massive weights are crashed together. Finally, one retreats in defeat. No, this is not a football game. It is the grandest rivalry in nature: Two rams fighting for the right to breed and pass along his genes to the next generation.

From the high alpine of the Rocky Mountains to the rocky peaks of the southwestern desert, bighorn sheep have adapted and survived in harsh conditions. However, their once huge numbers are declining due to their fiercest predator. It is not the mountain lion or the bobcat, but the human species.

Humans have the most profound effect on the environment. As our population continues to grow, so do the factors that bring about environmental degradation, including pollution, and urban growth. Environmental degradation is the process by which the environment is reduced in quantity and quality.

Urban Growth

During the westward expansion, around 1860, the human population in the U.S. was 31,443,321 and the population per square mile was 7.9. In 2000 the population was 281,421,906 and the population per square mile

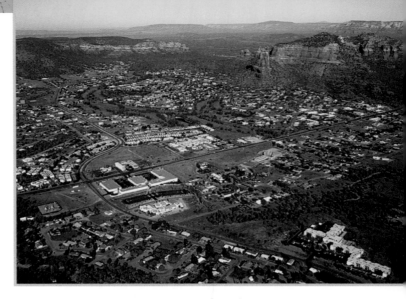

Aerial view of Sedona, Arizona

was 79.6. Since the size of the land is the same, this means that humans are encroaching on more and more land. Humans have the ability to change the course of a river for a new highway or destroy an ecosystem and clear huge tracts of land for apartment complexes and housing developments. However, we also have the ability to make wise land use decisions so we can meet our needs while preserving our natural heritage. This is possible because we understand how ecosystems work and what they need to remain viable.

Pollution

There are different kinds of pollution. Air pollution is produced by fuels that are burned to power industries, transport systems, and homes. To reduce this kind of pollution we should always remember to conserve energy.

Water pollution is caused by different factors. A common problem is excess fertilizers used in agriculture. Rain carries these excess fertilizers to streams and lakes. The algae in these streams and lakes grows excessively because of the fertilizers. When they die, they sink to the bottom where they decay. The decaying process uses the oxygen that other animals and plants need to survive.

Another kind of pollution is garbage. With more people comes more garbage and new places to put it. Landfills are filling quickly and new sites must be developed to accept the tons of garbage produced every day. When the land cannot sufficiently handle it, garbage is shipped out to sea to be dumped and become part of the food chain. To reduce this problem,

Factories produce smoke that pollutes the air.

Garbage disposal landfill

people can apply the three Rs of conservation: reduce, reuse and recycle. For example, we can reduce the amount of paper we use by using both sides of it, we can reuse things like bags and boxes, and we can take paper, plastic, and glass to the local recycling center.

Our use of the land has a constant effect on our natural resources, plants, animals, air, and water. Humans have done a lot to damage the environment. However, human intervention now helps to rehabilitate, recover, and preserve many areas of land that are vital to the survival of many different populations.

▷ **What are some things we can do to conserve the environment?**

How Does Mining Change the Environment?

The soil under your feet looks brown. The rocks are mostly gray. However, both hold a treasure chest of glittering colorful metals—gold, silver, aluminum, iron, copper, and many more.

People use these metals in many ways. Gold is made into jewelry and coins. Silver is, too. Silver is also used in photographic film and tableware.

Fly in an airplane. Ride in an automobile. Open a soft drink can. Squeeze a toothpaste tube. Marvel at fireworks. For all these things, you can thank aluminum. It's in each of these products.

Every large building, bridge, ship, train, and piece of machinery has iron in it—usually as part of steel.

Turn on your TV, your home's lights, a CD player. Electricity flowing through copper wires gets them going.

Clearly metals play an important part in our modern society. However, we pay a price for them—and not only

The easiest way to mine metals that are near the surface is to scrape the surface away. However, this leaves the land barren and often covered with dangerous chemicals.

in money. Since metal-containing rocks are buried in the ground, we must change the ground to get at them. If the rocks are near the surface, we simply carve away huge areas of land. This is called surface mining, open-pit mining, or strip mining.

In the United States alone, about 2,331 km² (900 mi²) of land has been cleared for mining. That's about three-fourths of the area of the entire state of Rhode Island.

Surface-mined land is loaded with substances that are harmful to living things. Rainwater flows easily over this kind of land and carries pollutants into nearby streams, rivers, and lakes. The wind picks up dust, which pollutes the air. In both cases, living things are harmed.

▷ **What is strip mining?**

Why It Matters

In nature, the size of a population is determined by the resources available and competition for those resources. However, populations today are also dependent on human actions.

People can do good and bad things to the environment. They can interfere with an ecosystem by damming up rivers, using pesticides, and cutting down trees. They can also preserve an ecosystem by passing laws that protect its animals and plants.

e-Journal Visit our Web site **www.science.mmhschool.com** to do a research project on the limiting factors of a species of your choice.

Think and Write

1. Identify two biotic and two abiotic limiting factors.

2. Explain what carrying capacity is using an example.

3. How does the decline in the bald eagle population affect other populations?

4. Make a list of ways you and your community affect your environment.

5. Critical Thinking Explain and evaluate some ways that humans affect ecosystems.

L·I·N·K·S

LITERATURE LINK

Read *The Eagles Are Back!* to learn about two eaglets named Ross and Betsey who were raised in a safe environment and then were returned to the wild. Try the activities at the end of the book.

MATH LINK

Find the range. Using the data on page B37, determine the range of young hatched and the range of insecticide in eggs from 1966 to 1981.

WRITING LINK

Expository Writing What resources have been exploited in your state? What are the results? Research the topic. Use the facts you find to write an essay. Then use scientific reasoning to end your essay with a recommendation, at the local and global levels, regarding this resource.

TECHNOLOGY LINK

Science Newsroom CD-ROM Choose *Keep Them Alive* to learn how sea turtles and other species get what they need to survive from their environment.

LOG ON Visit **www.science.mmhschool.com** for more links.

Coral Reefs

Rain Forests of the Sea

They're sometimes called "rain forests of the sea." That's because they're home for an amazing variety and number of creatures—up to a quarter of all the oceans' animals. They can take thousands of years to form. They grow in shallow, warm waters. Creatures smaller than your thumbnail build them, and they can be over a thousand miles long. What are they? Coral reefs!

A coral reef is built by millions of tiny animals called coral polyps. They live together in colonies, or groups. Coral polyps secrete a substance that hardens into skeletons. The hard skeletons build up reefs over time. Special algae live inside coral polyps. The algae produce food for the polyps. Coral reefs form only in shallow waters because the algae need sunlight to produce food.

A coral reef often looks like a sea garden because of its beautiful shades of orange, yellow, purple, and green. The colors come from the different algae and sea animals that live among the corals. Coral reefs provide food and shelter for thousands of ocean plants and animals, including hundreds of kinds of fish.

Some of the more unusual inhabitants of coral reefs include small fish and shrimp known as cleaners. Cleaners eat parasites from larger fish, such as barracudas and eels.

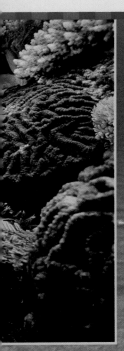

Coral reefs are endangered. As humans develop shorelines near the reefs, soil runs into coastal waters and smothers the fragile reefs. Pollution and destructive fishing practices also threaten reefs. Today many countries are trying to protect and save coral reefs.

What Did I Learn?

1. A coral reef is formed by

  A small pieces of rock.
  B sea shells.
  C tiny animals.
  D sand particles.

2. Coral reefs are endangered because of

  F severe storms.
  G human development. along shorelines.
  H lack of sunlight.
  J too many animals.

Red and yellow soft coral

Cleaner shrimp at work

LOG ON Visit www.science.mmhschool.com for more amazing stories and facts about ecosystems.

Chapter 5 Review

Vocabulary

Fill each blank with the best word or words from the list.

abiotic factor, B6
community, B11
ecology, B11
food chain, B18
mutualism, B25
niche, B12
omnivore, B21
population, B11
predator, B21
symbiosis, B24

1. A consumer that eats both plants and animals is called a(n) _____.

2. Water is an example of a(n) _____.

3. A(n) _____ includes all the members of a single species in a certain place.

4. Corn, elms, and armadillos are part of the _____ of the prairie ecosystem.

5. The study of how living and nonliving things interact in the same place is called _____.

6. All populations have a unique _____ in their habitat.

7. The relationship of _____ means that both populations benefit.

8. A(n) _____ is a consumer that hunts for its food.

9. A relationship between two organisms that lasts over a period of time is called _____.

10. You can trace how energy moves in a community with a(n) _____.

Test Prep

11. All of the following are abiotic factors in an ecosystem EXCEPT
   A water.
   B minerals.
   C bacteria.
   D soil.

12. A vulture is an example of a
   F predator.
   G scavenger.
   H carnivore.
   J all of the above

13. One example of a parasitic plant is
   A mistletoe.
   B an orchid.
   C a fir tree.
   D seaweed.

14. Surface mining can harm the environment when

    F trees are cut down to clear the land.

    G dust from surface-mined land causes air pollution.

    H rainwater washes pollutants into nearby streams.

    J all of the above

15. A relationship in which one organism benefits from another without helping or harming it is called

    A parasitism.

    B mutualism.

    C commensalism.

    D symbiosis.

Concepts and Skills

16. INQUIRY SKILL **Use Variables** Study the table below. Suggest a reason for the change in the eagle population.

Population Size			
Year	Grasslands (mi²)	Rabbits	Eagles
1960	10,200	101,000	1,050
1970	9,100	89,000	864
1980	8,200	78,000	782
1990	5,300	42,000	386
2000	5,140	41,900	378

17. Reading in Science Describe the sequence by which the Sun's energy is moved through a community.

18. Scientific Methods You discover that two of your ten ferns have a bacterium living on their stalks. If all the ferns are the same size and age, and you care for them all the same way, how do you determine if the fern and the bacterium have a symbiotic relationship? How would you determine if this relationship is an example of parasitism or mutualism?

19. Critical Thinking What is the relationship between herbivores and carnivores? Explain your answer in a paragraph.

20. Product Ads Advertisements for some products claim that the products are environmentally friendly. What does that mean? What are examples of products that are environmentally friendly and products that are not?

Did You Ever Wonder?

INQUIRY SKILL **Hypothesize** When wildlife are in a limited area and not free to roam, larger animals can be severely affected. What hypothesis explains this?

 LOG ON Visit www.science.mmhschool.com to boost your test scores.

CHAPTER 6

Ecosystems

Did You Ever Wonder?

In winter, these caribou leave their home on the tundra and migrate south, where they can find food and give birth to their young. In the summer they will return and usually find the same landscape they left in the winter.

INQUIRY SKILL Hypothesis Why can ecosystems remain unchanged year after year?

Cycles of Life

Vocabulary

evaporation, B50

condensation, B50

precipitation, B51

water cycle, B51

carbon cycle, B53

nitrogen cycle, B54

Get Ready

Have you ever walked in a grassy field early in the morning after a clear night? What did you observe about the grass? It was probably wet with dew. Where did all this water come from? It hadn't rained in the night. Dew comes from water in the air. How is water stored in the air? How does it change to dew?

Inquiry Skill

You infer when you form an idea from facts or observations.

Explore Activity

What Is the Water Cycle?

Materials

plastic food container with clear cover

small bowl or cup filled with water

small tray filled with dry soil

paper towel

100-W lamp (if available)

Procedure

1. Place the dry paper towel, the dry soil, and the bowl of water in the plastic container. Close the container with the lid.

2. **Observe** Place the container under a lamp or in direct sunlight. Observe every ten minutes for a class period. Record your observations.

3. Observe the container on the second day. Record your observations.

Drawing Conclusions

1. What did you observe the first day? What did you observe the second day?

2. **Infer** What was the source of the water? What was the source of the energy that caused changes in the container?

3. What happened to the water?

4. **FURTHER INQUIRY** **Infer** How did the water move? Use your observations to explain how water is recycled.

Main Idea Earth's systems recycle materials, such as water, carbon, and nitrogen.

What Is the Water Cycle?

What happens to rainwater after it falls? Does it simply vanish? Water moves from one part of the environment to another. It is not lost from an environment. In other words, water is recycled. How is this possible?

Here's how it happens. Heat from the Sun is absorbed by oceans, seas, lakes, streams, ponds, and even puddles. This heat makes the water evaporate and go into the air. **Evaporation** is the process in which a liquid changes into a gas.

As the *water vapor*, or water in its gas state, rises higher and higher into the atmosphere, it cools. When cooled enough, water vapor condenses into tiny water droplets. **Condensation** is

The Water Cycle

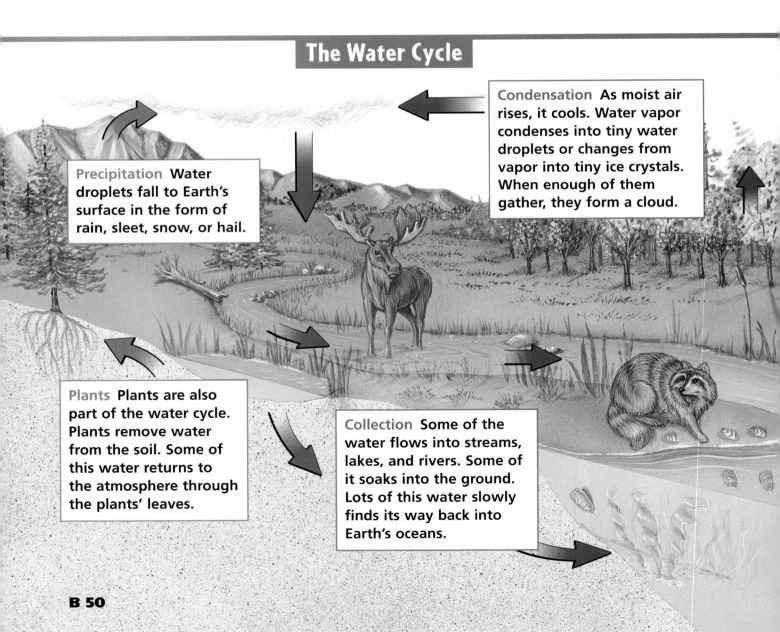

Condensation As moist air rises, it cools. Water vapor condenses into tiny water droplets or changes from vapor into tiny ice crystals. When enough of them gather, they form a cloud.

Precipitation Water droplets fall to Earth's surface in the form of rain, sleet, snow, or hail.

Plants Plants are also part of the water cycle. Plants remove water from the soil. Some of this water returns to the atmosphere through the plants' leaves.

Collection Some of the water flows into streams, lakes, and rivers. Some of it soaks into the ground. Lots of this water slowly finds its way back into Earth's oceans.

the process in which a gas changes into a liquid.

When enough water droplets gather, a cloud is formed. As more and more droplets gather, they become too heavy to stay in the air. They fall to Earth's surface as **precipitation**. Precipitation is any form of water particles—rain, sleet, snow, or hail—that falls to Earth.

On land some of the precipitation seeps into the ground and is stored as *groundwater*. Some of the water, however, lands on the *watershed*.

A watershed is an area on which water flows downhill to a common stream, lake, or river. This water is called *runoff*. It slowly finds its way back to the ocean. Here it absorbs heat and evaporates into the atmosphere again. The **water cycle** is the continuous movement of water between Earth's surface and the air, changing from liquid to gas to liquid.

READING **Summarize**

What are the stages of the water cycle?

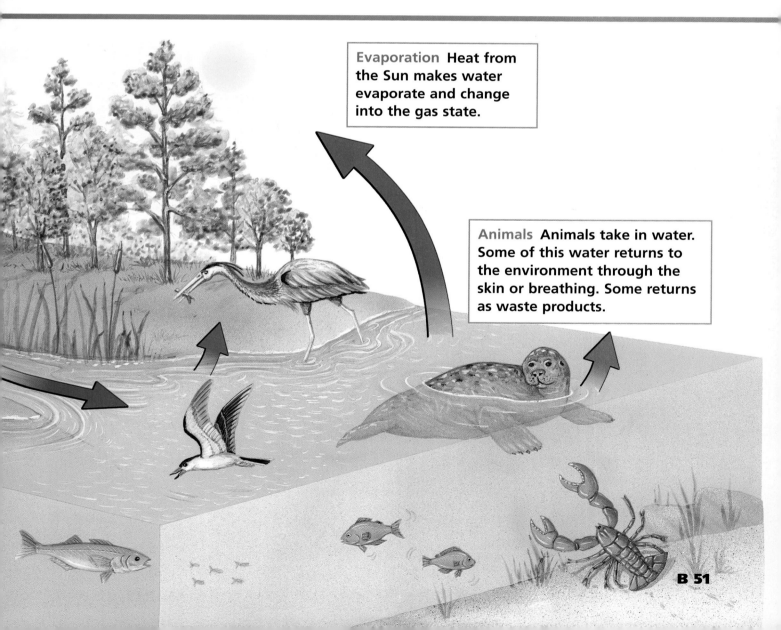

Evaporation **Heat from the Sun makes water evaporate and change into the gas state.**

Animals **Animals take in water. Some of this water returns to the environment through the skin or breathing. Some returns as waste products.**

What Is the Carbon Cycle?

Have you ever roasted marshmallows over a fire until the outsides turned black? Have you ever left bread in the toaster for so long that it burned? The "black" that you observe on burnt food is carbon.

Carbon is a very important element. It is one of the elements that make up all living things. It is found in the air as carbon dioxide and is used by plants in photosynthesis. It is found in many of the things we use every day, from fuel to chairs to nonstick pans.

The Carbon Cycle

Carbon enters the air when plants and animals decay. It enters the air when animals breathe out. It enters the air when fossil fuels such as coal, oil, gasoline, and natural gas are burned.

Plants During photosynthesis plants use the carbon from carbon dioxide to make sugars, starches, and proteins. They also give off oxygen, which is used by animals.

Car exhaust

Oil

Like water, carbon is recycled by nature. The process is called the **carbon cycle**. The carbon cycle shows the continuous transfer of carbon between the atmosphere and living things. Read the diagram to learn how nature does this.

▷ **What does the carbon cycle do?**

READING
Diagrams

1. When does carbon dioxide enter the air?

2. What happens to carbon when living things die?

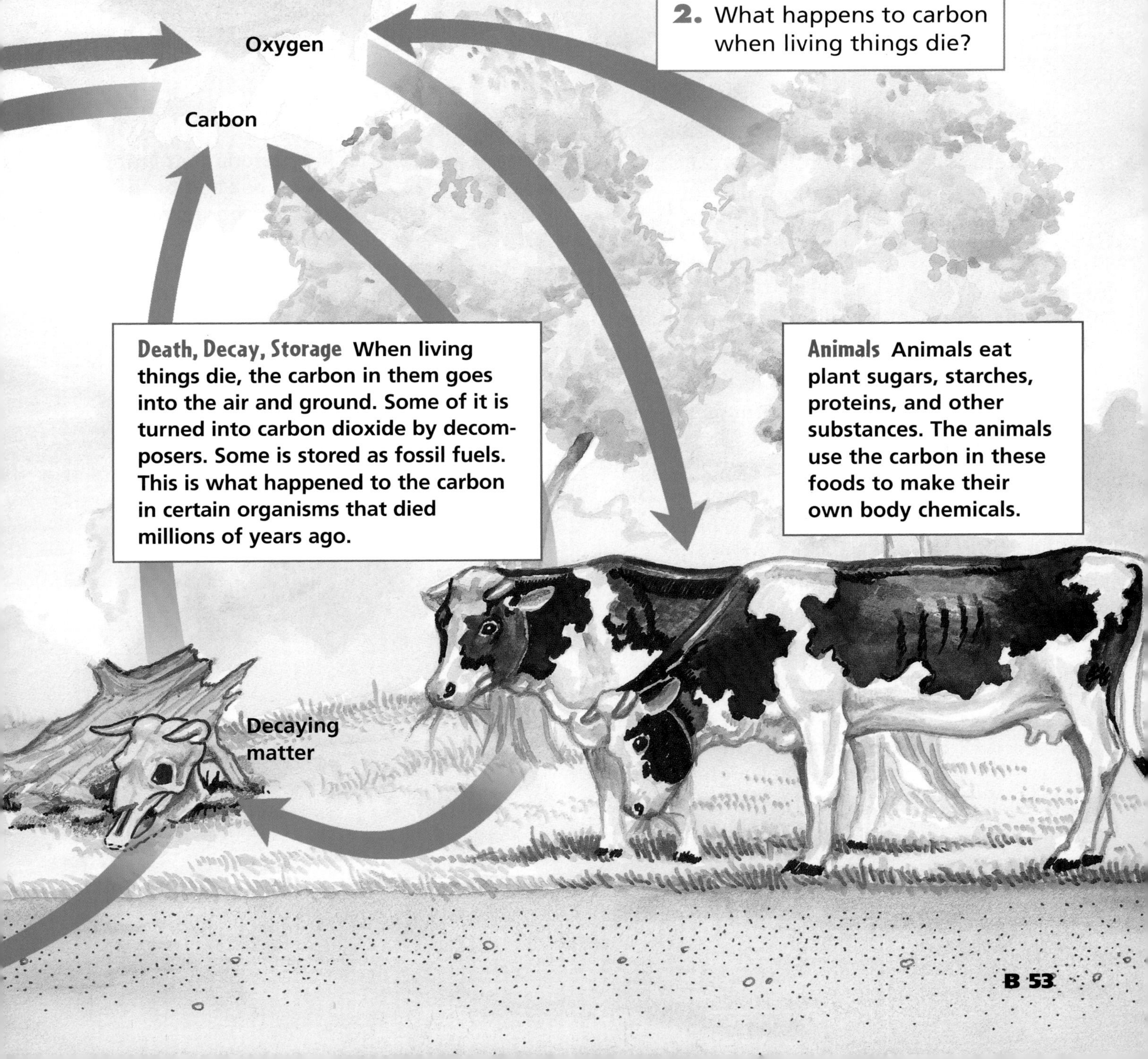

Oxygen

Carbon

Death, Decay, Storage When living things die, the carbon in them goes into the air and ground. Some of it is turned into carbon dioxide by decomposers. Some is stored as fossil fuels. This is what happened to the carbon in certain organisms that died millions of years ago.

Animals Animals eat plant sugars, starches, proteins, and other substances. The animals use the carbon in these foods to make their own body chemicals.

Decaying matter

B 53

How Is Nitrogen Recycled?

What do you need nitrogen for? When you eat meat, fish, cereal, or vegetables, you are taking in the nutrients that your body needs to make *proteins*. Proteins are a part of your muscles and many cell structures.

Among other things, proteins are rich in the element nitrogen. You need nitrogen to make parts of your body, such as muscles, nerves, skin, bones, blood, and digestive juices.

Since air is 78 percent nitrogen, you might think that you do not need to eat protein to get nitrogen. However, animals and plants cannot use the nitrogen that is in the air. Animals get nitrogen by eating proteins. Plants get nitrogen by absorbing it from the soil. Some plants even get nitrogen with the help of a special group of bacteria.

The way nitrogen moves between the air, soil, plants, and animals is called the **nitrogen cycle**.

▷ **What organisms are involved in the nitrogen cycle?**

The Nitrogen Cycle

Air Air is made up of about 78 percent nitrogen gas.

Nitrogen-Fixing Bacteria Some bacteria that grow on pea and bean roots give those plants the nitrogen they need. The bacteria turn nitrogen gas in the air to nitrogen-containing substances the plants can use to make their proteins.

Decomposers When plants die, decomposers in the soil break down the plant proteins. One product is the nitrogen-containing substance ammonia. Soil bacteria change ammonia into nitrites.

Ammonia

Diagrams

1. Compare the different ways various kinds of bacteria help in the nitrogen cycle.

2. How do pea and bean plants get the nitrogen they need?

Denitrifying Bacteria Some soil bacteria turn nitrates back into nitrogen gas.

Plants Plants absorb nitrates dissolved in water through their roots. The nitrogen is then used by the plant to make proteins.

Animals Animals eat plant proteins, or they eat other animals that eat plant proteins. Animal wastes contain nitrogen compounds.

Nitrites   **Nitrates**

Nitrogen compounds

Bacteria Certain bacteria can use nitrogen from the air to make nitrogen-containing substances called *nitrites*. Other bacteria can turn nitrites into *nitrates*—another group of nitrogen-containing substances.

Nitrites and ammonia

This dead tree is being decomposed by fungi, shown here, and microscopic bacteria.

How Are Trees Recycled?

How can a dead tree help living things? Even though the tree is dead, it is being turned into substances other organisms need to survive. Some of these organisms are other trees. The dead tree is providing elements for living trees. When these trees die, they will provide elements that other trees need. The cycling of matter is continuous. How does this happen?

An old, fallen tree is made of wood, bark, and other dead tree tissue. That tissue holds all sorts of complex chemical substances. Most of the chemicals are too complex to be used by other living things. They need to be broken down into simpler chemicals.

This is the job of the decomposers. They are organisms that recycle matter from dead organisms. Worms, crickets, cockroaches, bacteria, and fungi are decomposers. These organisms can

break down dead wood and other dead plant parts into carbon dioxide and ammonia. All living plants need carbon dioxide in order to make sugars. Ammonia is a simple substance that contains the element nitrogen. Nitrogen is extremely important for plants. No plant can live or grow without nitrogen. All organisms need nitrogen in order to make proteins.

Nitrogen is a chemical found in plant *fertilizers*. Fertilizers are substances used to add minerals to the soil. Some fertilizers are natural. These are decaying plants and animals, and animal wastes. Other fertilizers are made in factories. Both natural and artificial fertilizers contain nitrogen. The next time you go to a store that sells fertilizers, read the labels. You're sure to find nitrogen as one of the ingredients.

Composting

You can help nature recycle plant material by composting. Gardeners use compost to make soil more fertile. A good mixture for compost is three parts dry leaves and plant material, one part fresh grass clippings, and one part food scraps. Earthworms, insects, fungi, and bacteria break down the leaves, grass, and food scraps into compost. The compost contains nitrogen, phosphorous, and potassium, which enrich the soil.

As you'll soon discover, like water, nitrogen and carbon have their own cycles in nature. Earth is a closed system. With the exception of energy, almost nothing gets out or gets in. It is recycled.

▷ **How do decomposers recycle nutrients?**

Fertilizers sold in stores contain nitrogen. Nitrogen is an element plants need to grow and stay healthy.

Guaranteed Analysis

Total Nitrogen (N) 10%
Available Phosphate (P_2O_5) 10%
Soluble Potash (K_2O) 10%
The Plant Foods used in   Garden Food are Ammonium Sulfate, Triple Superphosphate and Potash. Also contained in Garden Food is the natural mineral limestone.

Food 10-10-10 is an agricultur...

QUICK LAB

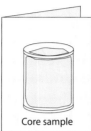

Soil Sample

FOLDABLES™ Make a Half-Book.
(See p. R 41.)

Core sample

BE CAREFUL! Do not touch the sharp edges of the can.

1. Go to a wooded area in a park or other location near your school. Find a patch of soft, moist soil.

2. Press a can, open side down, into the soil to get a core sample. You might have to gently rotate the can so it cuts into the soil.

3. **Observe** Carefully remove the core so it stays in one piece. Use your Half-Book to describe and draw the core.

4. **Infer** From top to bottom, what kind of matter does the core hold? In what order did the layers form?

5. **Infer** Which layer holds the most available nutrients? Explain.

Why Recycle?

Have you ever seen a paper bag with a symbol that says "Printed on recycled paper"? Why is this important?

The environment provides the materials people use to make products. Sunlight is an *inexhaustible resource*. The Sun will last for millions, if not billions, of years. Other resources, however, are not inexhaustible. The paper to make books, magazines, newspapers, and containers comes from the wood in trees. Metals mined from the ground are used to make cars, ships, pots and pans, appliances, and many other things. Glass is made from sand. Plastics are made from chemicals in oil found deep underground.

Wood, metals, sand, and oil are called *raw materials*. Raw materials are the building blocks of products.

Many raw materials, such as oil and metals, are *nonrenewable resources*. Earth's oil was formed millions of years ago. There's a limited amount of it. When it's gone, it's gone forever.

Certain other resources, such as plants and animals, are *renewable resources*. If trees are cut down for lumber and paper, more can be planted to replace them. Even so, trees take years to grow. This is why it is important to remember and practice the three Rs of conservation: reduce, reuse, and recycle.

> ▶ **Why is it important to recycle both renewable and nonrenewable resources?**

Garbage Thrown Away Daily in the United States

This graph shows the percent of different materials in garbage thrown away each day by each person in the United States.

READING Graphs

Let's say there are 280,000,000 people in the United States. Each person throws away 1.8 kg (4 lb) of garbage each day. How much garbage is thrown away by all the people each day?

L·I·N·K·S

Why It Matters

The environment will continue to provide all the things we need as long as we let it recycle the substances that make life possible. People can either help or hinder the process.

To help we can conserve raw materials by recycling them—just as nature recycles water, carbon, and nitrogen. Many communities have recycling programs to do this.

e-Journal Visit our Web site www.science.mmhschool.com to do a research project on the recycling and waste reduction laws in your state.

Think and Write

1. By what process does water move from oceans, lakes, rivers, and streams into the air?

2. What organisms turn a dead tree into substances that can be used by living trees?

3. Describe three ways that carbon dioxide gets into the air.

4. Name two substances that contain nitrogen.

5. **Critical Thinking** Many people use disposable products because they are safe and less expensive. What are the environmental costs of disposable products?

MATH LINK

Make a circle graph. Use the data from page B58. Calculate (in kilograms) how much of each type of garbage Americans produce every day.

ART LINK

Make a collage. Weigh the amount of garbage you throw away each day. Estimate how much of it is paper, glass, plastic, and food scraps. Represent this in a collage.

WRITING LINK

Writing That Compares How can people help save the environment by reducing waste, reusing, and recycling? Choose one product you use regularly and compare the three conservation strategies to see which one you think is the best for this product. Plan your writing in a three-column chart. Label each column with one of these labels: Reducing, Reusing, or Recycling. List the benefits of each for this product. Then use your chart to write an essay that compares.

TECHNOLOGY LINK

LOG ON Visit www.science.mmhschool.com for more links.

Recycling

Soccer practice just ended, and you're in a hurry. You gulp down your last drop of water. Now what do you do with the plastic bottle?

Your friends are waiting, so you toss the bottle in the nearest trash can. The plastic bottle will make its way to a landfill. There it could decorate the landscape for hundreds of years!

If you recycle the bottle instead, it could take on another life. Like many recycled materials, plastic can be made into other things. In recycling facilities, plastic bottles and jugs are sorted, chopped, and melted. Then the melted plastic is cooled and formed into beads. The beads can be used to make everything from picnic tables to carpets.

A lot of other things that we use can be recycled too. When a tree is turned into paper, it can start a loop that just keeps going. If you recycle things like paper, you're part of the loop. The paper that's recycled is shredded, boiled in water, and then made into paper again. So, when you use recycled paper, you're closing the loop.

And, don't let that banana peel slip into a landfill either. Even that can be recycled. If you have plants in your house or a yard, your family can make a compost pile of food scraps. In a few weeks, the scraps will decompose— break down into small pieces. The compost will make the soil rich in nutrients.

Recycle those water bottles!

We can all do our part. Let's all recycle!

Plastic bottles and jugs arrive at a recycling facility.

How long does it take trash to decompose?	
Paper and newspaper	4 weeks
Banana and orange peels	5 weeks
Plastic bags	20 years
Styrofoam cup	50 years
Aluminum can	100 years
Plastic bottle	700 years
Glass bottle	1,000,000 years

But there's something even better than recycling. It's throwing away less trash in the first place! At the grocery store, next time they ask, "Paper or plastic?" say, "Neither. I brought my own canvas bag."

 LOG ON Visit www.science.mmhschool.com to learn more about recycling.

What Did I Learn?

1. How are plastic bottles recycled?

A They are washed and refilled.

B They can't be recycled.

C They are chopped, melted, and made into beads.

D They are shredded.

2. As responsible citizens, you should do all of the following things. Which one is the most important recycling strategy?

F Cut down on waste in the first place.

G Recycle bottles and cans.

H Buy recycled products.

J Compost food scraps.

They are sorted and chopped into small pieces.

Recycled plastic beads come in different colors.

Biomes

Vocabulary

biome, B64

grasslands, B66

taiga, B67

tundra, B68

desert, B69

deciduous forest, B70

tropical rain forest, B71

Get Ready

What kinds of plants and animals live in the tropical rain forest? Are they the same as the ones that live in your community? Why do certain plants live in some areas and not others?

Soil varies greatly and is a distinctive factor in each area. Soil content can determine what plants and animals can live there.

Inquiry Skill

You observe when you use your senses to learn about an object or event.

Explore Activity

Why Is Soil Important?

Materials

washed sand

soil

hydrogen peroxide

2 plastic cups

2 plastic teaspoons

dropper

goggles

apron

Procedure

BE CAREFUL! Wear goggles and an apron.

1. Place 1 tsp. of washed sand in a plastic cup.

2. **Observe** Using the dropper, add hydrogen peroxide to the sand, drop by drop. Count each drop. Bubbles will form as the hydrogen peroxide breaks down any decayed matter.

3. **Communicate** Record the number of drops you add until the bubbles stop forming.

4. **Experiment** Repeat steps 1–3 using the soil.

Drawing Conclusions

1. Which sample—soil or sand—gave off more bubbles?

2. **Infer** Why was the sand used?

3. **Infer** Decayed materials in soil release their nutrients to form humus. The amount of humus in soil depends on the rate of decay and the rate at which plants absorb the nutrients. Which sample had more humus?

4. **FURTHER INQUIRY** **Infer** Use your observations to identify in which sample you could grow larger, healthier plants. Give evidence to support your answer.

Taiga

Deciduous forest

Tropical rain forest

What Is a Biome?

The land on Earth is divided into six major kinds of large eco-systems, called **biomes** (BIGH·ohmz). Each biome has its own kind of climate, soil, plants, and animals. Each biome can be found in different parts of the world. A desert biome is found in North America. Another is found in Africa. Still others are found in South America, Asia, and Australia. The map shows where Earth's six biomes are located around our planet.

▶ **What are the six major biomes?**

Taiga

Location: Mid- to high latitudes
Climate: Very cold winters, cool summers; about 50 cm (20 in.) of precipitation a year
Soil: Acidic, mineral-poor, decayed pine and spruce needles on surface
Plants: Mostly spruce, fir, and other evergreens
Animals: Rodents, snowshoe hares, lynx, sables, ermine, caribou, bears, wolves, birds in summer

Deciduous Forest

Location: Midlatitudes
Climate: Relatively mild summers and cold winters, 76–127 cm (30–50 in.) of precip-itation a year
Soil: Rich topsoil over clay
Plants: Hardwoods such as oaks, beeches, hickories, maples
Animals: Wolves, deer, bears, and a wide variety of small mammals, birds, amphibians, reptiles, and insects

Tropical Rain Forest

Location: Near the equator
Climate: Hot all year round, 200–460 cm (80–180 in.) of rain a year
Soil: Nutrient-poor
Plants: Greatest diversity of any biome; vines, orchids, ferns, and a wide variety of trees
Animals: More species of insects, reptiles, and amphibians than any place else; monkeys, other small and large mammals, including in some places elephants, all sorts of colorful birds

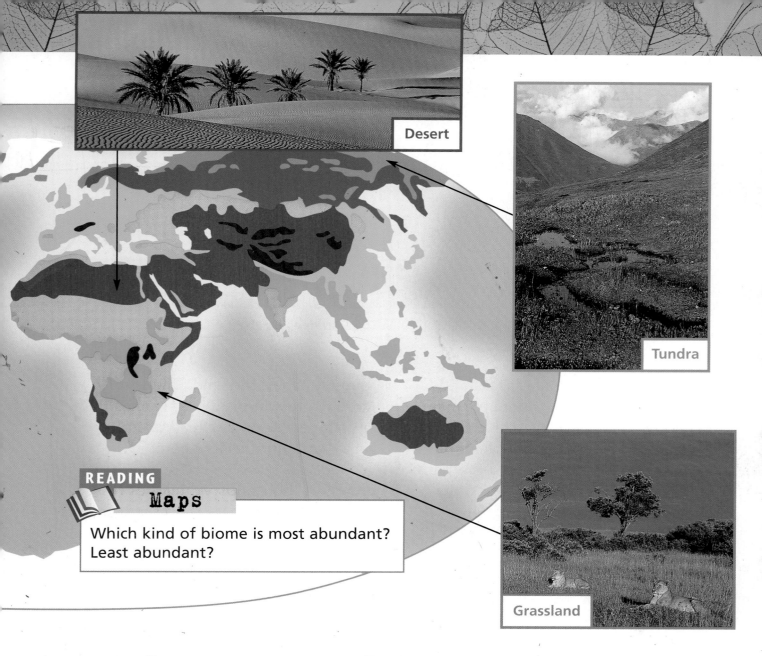

Desert

Tundra

Grassland

READING

📖 **Maps**

Which kind of biome is most abundant? Least abundant?

Desert

Location: Midlatitudes
Climate: Generally very hot days, cool nights; precipitation less than 4 cm (10 in.) a year
Soil: Poor in animal and plant decay products but often rich in minerals
Plants: None to cacti, yuccas, bunch grasses, shrubs, and a few trees
Animals: Rodents, snakes, lizards, tortoises, insects, and some birds. The Sahara in Africa is home to camels, gazelles, antelopes, small foxes, snakes, lizards, and gerbils.

Tundra

Location: High northern latitudes
Climate: Very cold, harsh, and long winters; short and cool summers; 10–25 cm (4–10 in.) of precipitation a year
Soil: Nutrient-poor, permafrost layer a few inches down
Plants: Grasses, wildflowers, mosses, small shrubs
Animals: Musk oxen, migrating caribou, arctic foxes, weasels, snowshoe hares, owls, hawks, various rodents, occasional polar bears

Grassland

Location: Midlatitudes, interiors of continents
Climate: Cool in winter, hot in summer; 25–75 cm (10–30 in.) of precipitation a year
Soil: Rich topsoil
Plants: Mostly grasses and small shrubs, some trees near sources of water
Animals: American grasslands include prairie dogs, foxes, small mammals, snakes, insects, various birds. African grasslands include elephants, lions, zebras, giraffes.

The lion lives on the savanna.

What Are Grasslands?

As the name tells you, **grasslands** are biomes where grasses are the main plant life. They are areas where rainfall is irregular and not usually plentiful.

Prairies, like the Blackland Prairie, are one kind of grassland. Called the "bread baskets" of the world, few temperate grasslands look as they did years ago. *Temperate* means "mild." It refers to grasslands such as those in the United States and Ukraine. Today many of these grasslands are covered with crops such as wheat, corn, and oats.

However, large parts of the world's tropical grasslands still look much as they have for hundreds of years. *Savannas* are grasslands that stay warm all year round. Their soil is not as fertile as that of temperate grasslands. However, they get more rain—about 86–152 cm (34–60 in.) a year.

The most famous savanna covers the middle third of Africa. Here the dust rises as countless hoofed animals thunder across the land. There are more hoofed animals in savannas than anywhere else on Earth. Graceful zebras and giraffes live here. Wildebeests travel in awesome herds of tens of thousands. Antelopes run from sprinting cheetahs. In the heat of the afternoon, lions rest in the shade of a thorny acacia tree. Nearby, hyenas prowl through the low grasses in search of dead or weak animals.

If you want to get a glimpse of a savanna while it still looks like this, you'd better do so soon. The land on savannas is being used more and more to graze domestic cattle. It won't be long until they replace the native animals, at least in unprotected parts of the savanna.

▷ **What are two types of grasslands? How are they different?**

What Is the Taiga Like?

Evidence indicates that about 15,000 years ago, huge fingers of ice, called glaciers, inched down from Earth's arctic regions. The ice was hundreds of feet thick. As it moved southward, it gouged great chunks of land out of northern Europe, Asia, and North America.

Some of the sediment carried by the glaciers dammed up streams, forming ponds and lakes. More lakes formed when the ice began to pull back. Holes dug by the glaciers filled with fresh water. These are the lakes and ponds of a cool, forested biome called the **taiga** (TIGH·guh).

Taigas are mostly conifer forests. They spread out over 11 percent of Earth's land. They are located in the upper latitudes of the Northern Hemisphere—in Alaska, Canada, Norway, Sweden, Finland, and Russia.

If you visit the taiga in the summer, you may hear the pleasant songs of birds. Many different kinds migrate to the taiga in summer. However, they head for warmer regions in the fall. You might also hear the whining sound of chain saws. That's because the taiga is a major source of lumber and pulpwood. Much of the lumber is used for making houses for the world's growing population. The pulpwood is turned into paper products of all kinds, such as the pages of this book.

READING Summarize
What are the main characteristics of the taiga?

Thousands of years ago, moving sheets of ice dug away the land of the taiga. The dug-out land would become some of its lakes and ponds. Today these bodies of water are guarded by great stands of evergreen trees.

The caribou, a member of the deer family, is among the large animals of the tundra.

What Is the Tundra?

Where is the ground frozen even in summer? Only 10–25 cm (4–10 in.) of precipitation fall here each year. Winters are long and icy cold. Summers are short and cool. Just a few inches below the surface, the ground is frozen all the time.

You can't find many plants taller than about 30 cm (12 in.). However, you have no trouble spotting weasels, arctic foxes, snowshoe hares, hawks, musk oxen, and caribou. Near the coast you see a polar bear. When warmer weather comes, mosquitoes by the millions buzz through the air. Where are you?

You are in the far north. You're between the taiga and the polar ice sheets. It could be northern Alaska or northern Canada. It could be Greenland or frigid parts of Europe or Asia. No matter which of these places you are in, you are in the same biome. This cold biome of the far north is the **tundra**.

Why is it so cold? Even in summer the Sun's rays only strike the tundra at a low, glancing angle. The Sun melts ice in the top layer of the soil. However, this water is kept from flowing downward by a layer of *permafrost*, or permanently frozen soil, underneath. The top layer of soil acts like a vast sponge for the melted ice.

Many tundra plants are wildflowers and grasses. The permafrost keeps large plants from developing the deep root systems they need. The growing season is very short—as little as 50 days in some places. The tundra soil is poor in nutrients, so the tundra cannot support large plants.

▷ **What are conditions in the tundra like?**

What Is the Desert Biome Like?

Sahara, Gobi, and Atacama stir up thoughts of adventures in strange, dangerous places. These are among the world's greatest **deserts**. A desert is a sandy or rocky biome, with little precipitation and little plant life.

Every continent has at least one desert. Africa has an enormous desert called the Sahara. Its sands dip down to the Atlantic Ocean in the west, the Mediterranean Sea to the north, and the Red Sea to the east. It is the largest desert on Earth, with an area of about 9,000,000 km^2 (3,500,000 mi^2). It is so large that it could cover all of the United States south of Canada. Picture those 48 states covered with sand and you get an idea of the size of the Sahara.

The Gobi Desert in China and Mongolia is the world's second largest desert. It is about 1,300,000 km^2 (500,000 mi^2). That's about twice the size of Texas.

You'll find the Atacama Desert in South America. It runs 968 km (600 mi) from the southern tip of Peru down through Chile. It lies between the Andes Mountains to the east and the Pacific Ocean in the west. The driest place on Earth is found in Arica, Chile. It averages only about 0.08 cm (0.03 in.) of rain a year. That's about the depth of six sheets of paper.

Few animals and plants live in deserts. Those that do are very hardy. They are well adapted to living in the desert.

▷ **How is the desert similar to and different from the tundra?**

To reach water, the roots of the mesquite plant (above) have been known to grow more than 79 m (260 ft) deep. That's the height of a 26-story building. Elf owls (left) build nests in cacti.

B 69

What Is a Deciduous Forest?

Have you ever seen leaves on trees change color in the fall? If you have, you have seen the **deciduous** (di·SIJ·ew·uhs) **forest** biome. This is a forest biome with many trees that lose their leaves each year.

This is where broad-leaved trees grow. Each autumn the leaves turn shades of yellow, orange, and red, giving the land beautiful colors. Then the leaves fall to the ground—which is what *deciduous* means—and decay. The dead leaves help make the soil rich and fertile.

Deciduous forests once covered most of the United States east of the Mississippi River and almost all of western Europe. Much has been cut down to make room for towns, cities, farms, and factories.

Many animals that once lived in deciduous forests still live on the land that was cleared for suburbs, farms, and towns. Chipmunks dart around bushes. Squirrels leap from branch to branch. Raccoons turn over trash cans. Skunks meander through the underbrush.

Birds like cardinals, robins, crows, and hawks, and insects such as bees still live in deciduous forests. Turn over a rock and you might discover a salamander or garter snake.

Many deciduous forests in the United States and Europe are now part of national parks or are in places where few people live. As long as they stay that way, people will be able to see the changing seasons.

▷ **What are the main characteristics of the deciduous forest?**

The trees of a deciduous forest shed their leaves each autumn, painting the land yellow, orange, and red.

Although you'd probably not enjoy an encounter with this family, it's an important part of the deciduous forest biome.

What Are Tropical Rain Forests?

In areas along and near Earth's equator are **tropical rain forests**. These biomes are hot and humid, with much rainfall. They support a wide variety of life.

The canopy of a tropical rain forest spreads like a huge umbrella. It is so thick that little sunlight ever reaches the ground. With little light few plants can grow on the ground. Most of the life is up high in the branches, where howler monkeys and purple orchids cling.

There are no tropical rain forests in North America or Europe. They are too far from the tropics. However, Central America, South America, India, Africa, Southeast Asia, Australia, and many Pacific Islands have rain forests. Each has its own kinds of plants and animals.

Millions of species of animals live in the world's tropical rain forests. Many species have yet to be discovered.

In Africa you might see a silverback gorilla or a troop of playful chimpanzees.

On the island of Borneo, you might see a red-haired, long-armed orangutan (uh·RANG·oo·tan) swinging through the trees.

The anaconda is the largest snake on the planet.

The world's most colorful birds—such as toucans (TEW·kanz) and quetzals (ket·SAHLZ)—live in tropical rain forests. Giant snakes like the 9 m (30 ft), 136 kg (300 lb) South American anaconda also live in tropical rain forests.

The world's tropical rain forests have been victims of people's needs for lumber, farmland, and minerals. Fortunately, people are now replanting and restoring tropical rain forests. Still, some of their millions of undiscovered plant and animal species may become extinct before they are discovered.

▷ **What are some characteristics of the tropical rain forest?**

Some of the most colorful birds on Earth, like this toucan, live in tropical rain forests like those of South America.

QUICK LAB

Freshwater Communities

FOLDABLES™ Make a Three-Tab Book. (See p. R 43.) Label the tabs as shown.

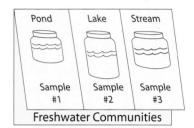

Pond	Lake	Stream
Sample #1	Sample #2	Sample #3

Freshwater Communities

1. **Obtain** from your teacher samples of pond, lake, or stream water taken at different locations. Use a different container for each sample. Record on the container the location each sample came from.

2. **Observe** Place a drop of water on a slide, and carefully place a coverslip over it. Use low power and high power to examine the slide under a microscope.

3. **Communicate** Sketch what you see under the appropriate tab of your Three-Tab Book.

4. **Interpret Data** What does this tell you about aquatic ecosystems?

What Are Water Ecosystems Like?

Temperature and precipitation differ among ecosystems on land. For Earth's watery ecosystems, the main difference is saltiness.

Lakes, streams, rivers, ponds, and certain marshes, swamps, and bogs tend to have little salt in them. They're all freshwater ecosystems. Oceans and seas are saltwater ecosystems.

In fresh water or salt water, organisms can be divided into three main categories. *Plankton* (PLANGK·tuhn) are organisms that float on the water. *Nekton* (NEK·tahn) are organisms that swim through the water. *Benthos* (BEN·thahs) are bottom-dwelling organisms.

Freshwater Organisms

Many plants live in the shallow waters of lakes, ponds, and other bodies of fresh water. If you were to wade here, you might get your feet tangled in cattails, bur reeds, wild rice, and arrowheads. You might also spot a frog, a turtle, or maybe a crayfish.

Farther out, where the water gets deeper, are microscopic plankton like algae and protozoa.

Look beneath the surface, and nekton come into view. There might be large trout or other game fish. All the way to the bottom, an aquatic worm might be burrowing into the mud.

Saltwater Organisms

Like the freshwater ecosystem, the marine, or ocean, ecosystem is divided into several sections.

The shallowest is the *intertidal zone*. There the ocean floor is covered and uncovered as the tide goes in and out. Crabs burrow into the sand so they won't be washed away. Mussels and barnacles attach themselves to rocks.

The open ocean is divided into two regions. The first region is up to 200 m (656 ft) deep. In this upper region are many kinds of fish and whales. The world's largest animals—the 150-ton blue whales—live here.

The lower region goes from 200 m (656 ft) to the ocean bottom—perhaps 10.5 km (6.5 mi) down. At depths greater than about 1,000 m (3,281 ft), there is no sunlight. It is completely black!

Photosynthetic organisms, like algae, can only live where there is sunlight. They are found in the inter-tidal zone and in waters up to about 100 m (328 ft) deep. Many fantastic creatures live on the dark ocean bottom. Some of these fish "light up" like underwater fireflies. Other bottom-dwelling fish are blind. There are even bacteria that live in boiling water where fiery lava seeps out of the sea floor.

▶ **What are two-water ecosystems? How do they differ?**

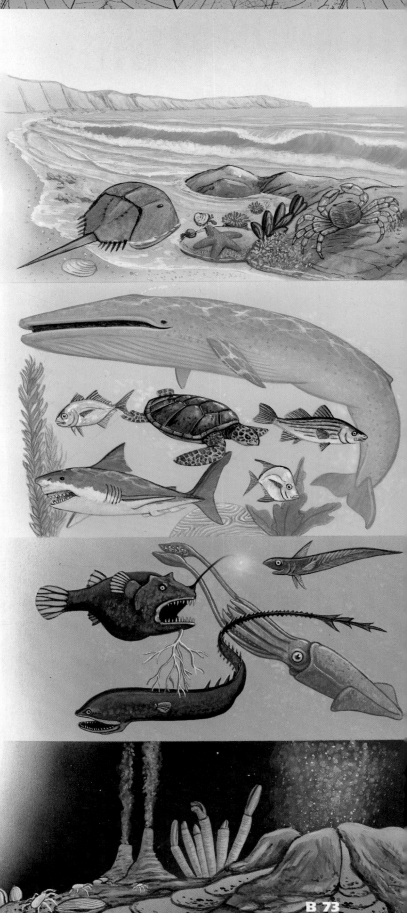

The types of animals you see in the ocean change as you go deeper.

Will the remaining whale populations survive? Will the eerie song of the humpback no longer be heard?

Can Humans Change Water Ecosystems?

People started hunting whales for their meat and oil at least 4,000 years ago. However, back then oceans held so many whales that hunting didn't have much effect on their populations.

As the centuries passed, however, whale hunting increased. So did the technology of finding and killing these gentle mammals. By 1850 American whalers alone accounted for the killing of 10,000 a year.

Over the next 100 years, new technologies made whale hunting easier and more efficient. In 1962 alone 66,000 whales were killed. The whales could not reproduce fast enough to replace those that were being killed. Many species, like blue whales, humpbacks, bowheads, and right whales, became threatened with extinction.

The whales were being used for human and animal food, oil for lamps, and fertilizer. However, there were other sources of such products. Recognizing this and the danger to whale populations, the major whaling countries formed the International Whaling Commission (IWC) in 1946.

In 1971 the United States banned its citizens from whaling for profit or even buying products made from whales. By the 1990s the IWC had succeeded in getting whaling countries to reduce or stop hunting threatened whales.

How have humans affected the whale population?

Why It Matters

The world's biomes remain constant as long as their climates and populations do not change greatly. However, climates and populations change naturally. Also, human activity has affected both populations and climates. Changes in a biome can affect the kinds of plants and animals that can live there. It can also affect people's lifestyles. It is important to know if, how, and why these factors are changing before we make irreversible changes.

e-Journal Visit our Web site www.science.mmhschool.com to do a research project on climate changes caused by human activity.

Think and Write

1. Describe the taiga biome in terms of its climate, soil, and inhabitants.

2. How do organisms found in desert and tundra biomes adapt to their environments?

3. Explain why few plants live on the floor of tropical rain forests.

4. Briefly describe the two types of aquatic ecosystems.

5. **Critical Thinking** Choose one biome, and explain how a change in its climate might affect its populations.

L·I·N·K·S

MATH LINK

Find the range. The monthly precipitation in a tropical rain forest in a year is 9 in., 6 in., 4 in., 21 in., 17 in., 8 in., 0 in., 3 in., 7 in., 25 in., 15 in., and 15 in. What is the range of the annual precipitation?

LITERATURE LINK

Read *Antarctica*, the story of the coldest continent on Earth. Try the activities at the end of the book.

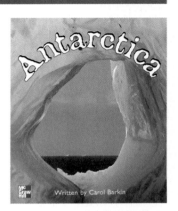

Written by Carol Barkin

WRITING LINK

Personal Narrative What would you do if the biome where you lived suddenly got warmer or colder? How would you adapt if the precipitation suddenly increased or decreased? Write a personal narrative about an adventure you might have if the biome where you lived suddenly changed. Use the "I" point of view to tell your story.

TECHNOLOGY LINK

 LOG ON Visit www.science.mmhschool.com for more links.

Agriculture

Humans have adapted to live in every biome on Earth, from the tropical rain forests to the deserts. But we have adapted our environment to fit our own needs, too.

Until about ten thousand years ago, our ancestors were continually on the move. They relied on the food they could gather and the animals they could hunt. Then they learned how to take the seeds of plants and grow their own food. Agriculture was born.

After that, humans began to settle down in one place and to domesticate animals. Attaching plows to horses and oxen let us farm larger areas and grow more crops.

Growing the same plant in the same area year after year exhausts the soil, draining its nutrients. Cutting down forests to make room for crops causes soil to erode. Planting the same plant in large areas encourages certain species of insects and weeds. These opportunists quickly become pests, harming other species, sometimes to the point of extinction.

It takes centuries for soil to become fertile. When too many trees are cut down in a forest, the soil washes off the land into rivers like this one.

New computerized irrigation systems use less water and chemicals. This saves money. It also reduces the amount of chemicals seeping into the ground.

To make farming easier, we invented steel plows and then tractors to help plant and harvest crops. We cleared forests, filled wetlands, and let cattle graze on grasslands.

We redirected rivers to bring water to dry deserts, destroying natural habitats. We also began to use chemicals to fertilize crops and kill the bugs and weeds. These chemicals seep into the soil and groundwater, and many pests become immune to the toxins.

Today, agricultural practices are changing. Some farmers are using organic, or chemical-free, methods to grow crops. These methods are safer, even though an acre will only produce half as many organic crops as regular ones. Some farmers are using natural pest control that uses insect predators such as spiders and ladybugs to kill pests.

Computerized irrigation systems are cutting down on the amount of water and chemicals used. These techniques and new ones are letting us grow food in smarter ways—ways that are protecting our planet.

Write About It

1. What are two technological advancements in agriculture, and how have they changed farming?

2. How can farming damage the land?

LOG ON Visit www.science.mmhschool.com to learn more about agriculture.

How Ecosystems Change

Get Ready

Before May 18, 1980, the area around Mount Saint Helens in the state of Washington was decorated with wildflowers and beautiful groves of Douglas fir and western hemlock trees. Animals of many kinds made their home here. Then the mountain exploded. What happened to the community? How did this ecosystem change?

Inquiry Skill

You predict when you state possible results of an event or experiment.

Explore Activity

How Do Ecosystems Change?

Procedure

1. **Observe** Examine the photograph.
2. **Communicate** Describe what you see.

Drawing Conclusions

1. **Infer** What happened to this farm after the owner left and moved to the city?

2. **Infer** Think about how this farm might have looked ten years ago. What kinds of plants lived there then?

3. **Interpret Data** How can one ecosystem be changed into another?

4. **Compare** what you think will happen to the abandoned farm with what happened at Mount Saint Helens. In what ways would the changes in ecosystems be similar? In what ways would they be different?

5. **FURTHER INQUIRY** **Predict** Think of another ecosystem that might be changed by nature. Think of an ecosystem that might be changed by humans. Describe how such ecosystems might continue to change over time.

Main Idea Ecosystems go through both slow and sudden changes.

How Do Ecosystems Change?

Changes happen everywhere on Earth. They can occur in your backyard. They can happen in an empty city lot or on one of its abandoned streets. If given a chance, nature will change an existing ecosystem or produce a new one. How does nature change an abandoned farm's field into a flourishing forest?

In the first year, a community of crabgrass, insects, and mice invades the field where corn or another crop once grew.

Abandoned cities of Angkor in Cambodia became covered by jungle.

Tall weeds, such as asters, ragweed, and goldenrod, and tall grasses grow among the crabgrass. The crabgrass can't easily survive in the shade cast by the taller weeds. It begins to die out in the second and third year. Rabbits and seed-eating birds move in.

The hot, dry field of tall weeds provides a perfect environment for

From Farmland to Forest

Abandoned Farm—First Year

Second and Third Years

pine seeds to sprout. By the fourth year, pine trees begin to grow and shade the weeds, which begin to die out. More birds join the community, as do small mammals like opossums and skunks.

A pine forest has replaced the old farm field within twenty-five years. The number of new pine seedlings drops, however, because they can't grow in the shade. Seeds of deciduous trees, such as maple, hickory, and oak, sprout and take root. Larger animals like raccoons and foxes begin to visit.

The forest is now mostly deciduous trees. These trees are the habitats of many different kinds of birds and small animals, such as squirrels. Deer, raccoons, and foxes also live in the forest.

▶ **How can an abandoned farm become a deciduous forest ecosystem?**

Four to Six Years Later

Twenty-Five Years Later

One Hundred Years Later

How Do Communities Change?

The abandoned farm field you just read about gave way to short crabgrass, then tall grasses and shrubs. Later, pine trees and, finally, deciduous trees grew there. Scientists call the gradual replacement of one community by another **ecological succession**.

Ecological succession can begin in two different kinds of places. It can begin where a community already exists—such as in an abandoned farm field. Ecological succession in a place where a community already exists is called *secondary succession*.

Ecological succession can also happen where there are few, if any, living things. This is called *primary succession*. Primary succession can begin where communities were wiped out. Such places would include land swept clean by a volcanic eruption or forest fire. It can also begin where communities never existed before, such as on a new island that rises out of the sea.

Mount Saint Helens

Explore what happened to Mount Saint Helens in the state of Washington shortly after May 18, 1980.

Mount Saint Helens had just erupted. The blast from the volcano knocked down thousands of trees. The whole area was covered knee-deep with hot volcanic ash and finely smashed-up rock.

The landscape was different shades of gray as far as you could see. No spot of green greeted your eyes, not even a blade of grass. If you didn't

Ecological Succession on Mount Saint Helens

1 year The rose-purple flowers of fireweed announced that life was returning to the destroyed land.

4 years Seedlings of Douglas fir trees began to take root in the rubble of the volcano.

know better, you might have thought you were on the Moon.

A year passes. You return to the slopes of Mount Saint Helens expecting to see unbroken stretches of rock and stumps of dead trees. However, something has happened in the year you were gone. Wind and rain have cleared some of the ash and dust, especially from steep slopes. The wind has also blown in some seeds and fruits from nearby forests. You see a scattering of rose-purple objects among the charred and fallen tree trunks. They are the flowers of a plant called fireweed. It gets its name from the fact that it is often the first plant to grow after a forest fire.

Scientists would call the fireweed a **pioneer species**. That's because it is the first species to be living in an otherwise lifeless area. You notice that the blooming of fireweed has attracted animals, such as insects and an occasional insect-eating bird. A new community, called a **pioneer community**, is beginning to thrive around Mount Saint Helens.

You return in 1984 and almost step on a little green shoot. You bend down and take a closer look. The shoot has little needlelike leaves. It is the sprout of a Douglas fir tree. Its seed was probably blown here from a forest miles away.

Now picture the land around Mount Saint Helens 100 or 200 years in the future. It is covered with a dense forest of evergreens. The forest is much like the one that spread around it before that explosive day in 1980.

▶ **How does ecological succession change communities?**

11 years Young fir trees grow tall 11 years after the blast.

13 years Fir tree revegetation was further along 13 years after the eruption.

B·83

What Happens to Pioneer Communities?

Are the first organisms in a pioneer community always plants? In some places the answer is no. This is usually the case in newly formed, fiery volcanic islands that rise from the sea. Here the pioneer community is often made up of bacteria, fungi, and algae. Over many years these organisms slowly break down the volcanic rock into soil.

What happens when there is enough soil, and other conditions are right for plants to grow? A seed blown to the island by the wind or dropped by a passing bird will take root. The new plant, and others like it, will gradually spread over the land.

During their life cycles, plants will die and further enrich the soil.

Perhaps a coconut will drift ashore. When it germinates, its roots will find a good supply of nutrients. A coconut palm will spring up, and a new island paradise will be created.

Climax Communities

More years will pass—perhaps hundreds of them. The climate of the island will remain almost unchanged. Its community will grow. Its populations will become balanced and stable. Few new animals and plants will arrive. Few will leave. Ecological succession will slow down or stop altogether. This is a **climax community**, a final stage of succession. This community will stay largely unchanged unless some major event occurs.

Stages of Succession

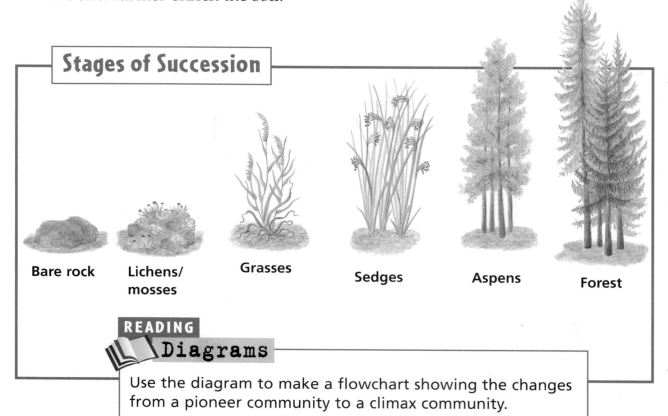

Bare rock   Lichens/mosses   Grasses   Sedges   Aspens   Forest

READING Diagrams

Use the diagram to make a flowchart showing the changes from a pioneer community to a climax community.

What kind of event could change an entire ecosystem? A hurricane may sweep across the island. The volcano that created it might erupt again. People might come and build hotels or introduce new plants or animals. The climate might change. Then the processes of ecological succession would begin all over again. Another climax community would eventually develop. It might—or might not—be the same as the earlier climax community.

▷ **What is the difference between a pioneer community and a climax community?**

The volcano Kilauea erupting on the island of Hawaii.

QUICK LAB

Predicting Succession

FOLDABLES Make a Four-Tab Book. (See p. R 44.) Label the tabs as shown. Record your answers on your Four-Tab Book.

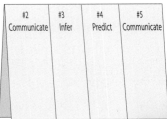

| #2 Communicate | #3 Infer | #4 Predict | #5 Communicate |

1. **Observe** Identify an area near you where you think ecological succession is taking place.

2. **Communicate** Describe the area. List the evidence you have that indicates ecological succession is taking place.

3. **Infer** Do you think the succession will be primary or secondary? Explain.

4. **Predict** In what order do you think new species will colonize the area? Explain the reasons for your predictions.

5. **Communicate** Describe the climax community that you think will eventually live in the area. Give reasons for your conclusion.

What's Living on Surtsey?

In 1963 the island of Surtsey, near Iceland, was formed from a volcano. Between 1963 and 1996, at least 45 types of plants were seen growing there. Several kinds of birds, such as snow buntings, were also found raising their young on the island. Flying insects have also been found there. Scientists expect that more types of plants and birds will live on Surtsey in the future.

▷ **How is Surtsey an example of ecological succession?**

Surtsey, a volcanic island, rose from the sea near Iceland in 1963.

By 1996 many plants and birds lived on Surtsey.

Inquiry Skill BUILDER

SKILL Infer

Comparing Ecosystems in Volcanic Areas

In this activity you will collect data and infer about the ecosystems of two volcanic areas.

Data are different kinds of facts. They might include observations, measurements, calculations, and other kinds of information. Scientists collect data about an event to better understand what caused it, what it will cause, and how it will affect other events.

What do these data tell the scientist? The scientist first organizes the data in some way—perhaps a table, chart, or graph. The scientist then studies the organized data and makes inferences. To infer means to form an idea from facts or observations. In this case you will infer about which plants will return to a volcanic area.

Materials
research books
Internet

Procedure

1 Collect data on two volcanic areas, such as Mount Saint Helens and the Soufriere Hills volcano on the island of Montserrat or the active volcanoes of Hawaii. Organize the data.

2 **Communicate** Describe the sequence of events that has taken place.

3 **Interpret Data** Draw a conclusion about why certain plants return when they do.

Drawing Conclusions

1 In what ways is succession in the two areas alike? In what ways is it different?

2 **Infer** Why is the succession in these two areas similar or different?

3 **Infer** What abiotic factors must you consider when drawing conclusions? What biotic factors must you consider?

How Do Populations Survive Earth's Changes?

Earth is constantly changing. About 18,000 years ago, great sheets of ice moved deep into the heartland of what is now the United States. Vast ice sheets also covered much of Europe and parts of South America. Sea levels dropped as more and more water froze. New land was exposed. Earth was a cold place.

Slowly Earth began to warm up. The ice melted. Sea levels rose. Coastal land became flooded.

These kinds of changes have occurred no fewer than seven times during the past 700,000 years. Scientists call these cold periods *ice ages*.

Earth has also changed in other ways. Over millions of years, continents have moved north and south, east and west. Huge mountain-sized rocks have crashed into Earth. Volcanoes have poured gases and dust into the air.

Each of these events has had an effect on living things. Some organisms have survived these changes, while others have died out, or become extinct. Why have some of these organisms vanished while others survived?

To answer this, let's look at the age of the dinosaurs. Fossils from about 65 million years ago suggest that dinosaurs shared the land with many other animals. These animals included frogs, snails, insects, turtles, snakes, and some small furry mammals. Plants of all kinds grew everywhere. The seas were full of organisms like fish, sea urchins, clams, and algae.

Dinosaur footprints

Scientific evidence suggests that a meteorite up to 10 km (6 mi) in diameter struck Earth from outer space. One theory states that the impact created a huge explosion. It gouged out a crater 64 km (40 mi) across and threw huge amounts of dust into the sky. The dust may have hung in the sky for months, even years. Sunlight was probably blocked from reaching the ground.

Plants needing lots of sunlight may have died out. That means that the large plant-eating dinosaurs could not get enough food. They would have died out. The large dinosaurs preying on plant eaters would have also died out. It may have been that every animal weighing more than about 121 kg (55 lb) became extinct.

However, many of the smaller animals could have survived. They needed less food to live. They could have moved more easily from habitat to habitat. They would no longer have been in competition with the dinosaurs. They would have been free to grow in size and variety. Possibly this is how a world once ruled by dinosaurs became ruled by mammals.

▷ **How do changes on Earth affect organisms?**

Dinosaurs became extinct about 65 million years ago. Scientists can study them today, however, by searching for fossils, such as footprints and skeletons.

What Do Fossils Tell Us About Changes in the Environment?

Scientists have developed hypotheses to solve the following mystery.

- Scientists gathering fossils in Italy make a discovery. About six million years ago, fish and other sea creatures disappeared from the Mediterranean Sea.

- Other fossils from a slightly later period reveal that horselike animals from Africa arrived in Europe.

- The fossil of an ancient African hippopotamus is found on an island in the middle of the Mediterranean.

- Fossil palm trees of the same age are dug up in Switzerland.

- Then there is another surprising discovery. Five-million-year-old fossils of fish turn up in the Mediterranean area.

What could have gone on back then to have these clues make sense? One theory is called *plate tectonics*.

Earth's crust is made up of moving plates—pieces of crust. About six million years ago, two plates—the African and the Eurasian—collided. The continents of Africa and Europe bumped into each other. This happened at what is now the Strait of Gibraltar. This collision created a natural dam between the Atlantic Ocean and the Mediterranean Sea.

Without a source of water from the ocean, the sea dried up in perhaps as little as 1,000 years. The Mediterranean Sea became a desert. The sea's fish and other marine life died out. Animals from Africa migrated across the desert to Europe. Palm trees sprouted in Switzerland.

Then about five million years ago, the dam began to crumble. A gigantic waterfall poured water into the desert. It carried many kinds of marine life from the Atlantic Ocean. The Mediterranean became a sea again.

READING Summarize
How did changes in the Mediterranean affect populations?

6 million years ago

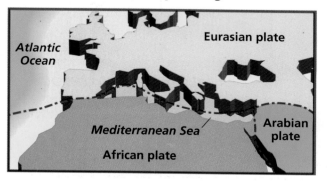

Present day

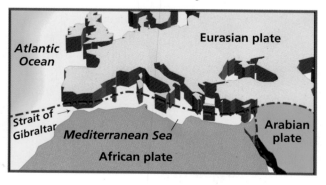

L·I·N·K·S

Why It Matters

Once an ecosystem is disturbed it begins to change until a stable climax community is reached. A climax community is an area where biotic and abiotic factors interact to maintain a stable environment.

Ecosystems change and recover from natural disasters and human activities in predictable ways. Understanding of succession and climax communities can prevent human-made ecological disasters and can help us set the right conditions to help environments recover faster.

e-Journal Visit our Web site **www.science.mmhschool.com** to do a research project on what fossils can tell us about environmental changes. Find a specific example.

Think and Write

1. Describe how an abandoned farm field becomes a deciduous forest.

2. Give an example of a pioneer and a climax community.

3. List the evidence that supports the conclusion that the Mediterranean Sea once dried up.

4. **Infer** How might a volcanic eruption affect an ecosystem?

5. **Critical Thinking** How would succession be affected if animals did not return to an area after a fire?

LITERATURE LINK

Read *Wildfire* to learn about the true story of a wildfire that destroyed 5,000 acres of land in New York. Try the activities in the back of the book.

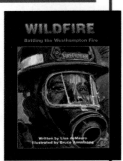

WRITING LINK

Expository Writing How do ecosystems change over time? Research what happened to Angkor. What was the culture like? Why did the people leave their city? Write a research report on your findings.

MATH LINK

Divide by one-digit numbers. Iceland has an area of 39,756 mi. Surtsey has an area of 2 mi. How many times larger is Iceland than Surtsey?

TECHNOLOGY LINK

Science Newsroom CD-ROM Choose *From the Ground Up* to learn how ecosystems change.

LOG ON Visit **www.science.mmhschool.com** for more links.

Chapter 6 Review

Vocabulary

Fill each blank with the best word or words from the list.

biome, B64
carbon cycle, B53
climax community, B84
desert, B69
ecological succession, B82
evaporation, B50
pioneer community, B83
precipitation, B51
taiga, B67
tundra, B68

1. Part of the soil of the _____ is frozen all year round.

2. The gradual change from one community to another is called _____.

3. The _____ shows the continuous transfer of carbon between living and nonliving things.

4. The _____ has many evergreen trees.

5. A(n) _____ is made up of the first organisms to colonize an area.

6. Sleet and snow are examples of _____.

7. When ecological succession slows down, a(n) _____ has formed.

8. A deciduous forest is an example of a(n) _____.

9. The process in which a liquid becomes a gas is called _____.

10. The Gobi and Mojave are examples of _____.

Test Prep

11. All of the following are abiotic factors in an ecosystem EXCEPT
  A water.
  B minerals.
  C bacteria.
  D soil.

12. A vulture is an example of a
  F predator.
  G scavenger.
  H carnivore.
  J all of the above

13. Plants absorb nitrogen
  A from the soil.
  B from the atmosphere.
  C from the Sun.
  D from insects.

14. A _____ is an example of a biome.
  F pond
  G bacteria
  H grassland
  J mammal

15. Scientists call _____ a pioneer species.

   A grasses

   B fir trees

   C fireweed

   D fallen tree trunks

Concepts and Skills

16. Reading in Science Summarize the steps in the nitrogen cycle.

17. Scientific Methods You discover that there are no fossils of dinosaurs above a certain layer of rock, but there are below it. The rock in this layer has more in common with rocks from space than with Earth rocks. Hypothesize how these two discoveries may be linked.

18. INQUIRY SKILL **Infer** What can you infer from the data below?

Pond Populations and Acid Content

Acid	Yellow Perch	Brown Trout	Salamanders	Mayflies
High	23	6	2	0
Medium	28	11	7	2
Low	36	18	10	14

19. Critical Thinking How might a change in the biome you live in affect your way of life?

20. Decision Making Is it important to recycle the waste you produce? Why or why not?

Did You Ever Wonder?

INQUIRY SKILL **Observe** Choose an area near your school or in your neighborhood. Determine how materials in this area are recycled by nature. Would you add or remove any elements to help the natural recycling process?

LOG ON Visit www.science.mmhschool.com to boost your test scores.

Dr. Catherine Toft

POPULATION ECOLOGIST

Desert bee fly

Dr. Catherine Toft is a population ecologist. Population ecology is the study of populations in nature. "It focuses on how numbers of individuals in a population change through time or vary from place to place," Dr. Toft says. Toft explains that a population is a group of individuals of the same type that mate within the group and produce offspring.

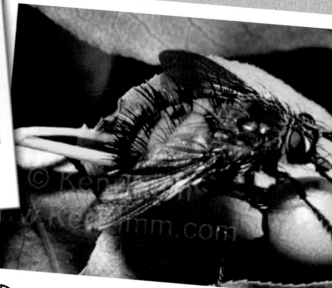

Desert Bee Fly

Dr. Toft loves discovering new things about nature. She spends most of her time in the field. She studies her subjects in their natural environments. "I study desert plants and desert insects," Dr. Toft says.

One of Dr. Toft's favorite subjects is the desert bee fly. The males gather in groups, called leks, to fight over the females. "These leks are in the same place every year even though the male flies live only one season. It is a mystery how the flies know to come to the same place every year, which looks like any other place in the sand dunes where they live."

Dr. Toft's work can help change the way we think about nature. "I hope that I can help people live lives that are more environmentally healthy."

TOP 5 Longest-Living Animals

Do you want to work with living things? A population ecologist such as Dr. Toft studies how long organisms live. Here are the animals that live the longest and the oldest known age for each.

1. Giant tortoise: 200 years
2. Human: 122 years
3. Sturgeon (a type of fish): 100 years
4. Blue whale and golden eagle: 80 years
5. African elephant: 77 years

Write About It

1. What is a lek?
2. Why do leks fascinate Dr. Toft?

LOG ON Visit www.science.mmhschool.com to learn more about the work of population ecologists.

Ecosystem Discovery

Your goal is to invent and describe a new ecosystem.

What to Do

1. Imagine you are an explorer. You have found the world's last unexplored ecosystem. Give your ecosystem a name.

2. Describe this new ecosystem. Write about the plants and animals there. Tell what each one needs to survive.

3. Draw a picture of your ecosystem.

Analyze Your Results

1. Tell how each plant and animal gets what it needs to survive in your ecosystem.

2. What nonliving things help plants and animals survive in your ecosystem?

3. Draw an energy pyramid to show how energy moves in your ecosystem. What belongs at the bottom of the pyramid? At the top?

Will Succession Succeed?

Your goal is to identify a place where ecological succession is taking place.

What to Do

1. Write a short paragraph describing what ecological succession is.

2. Think of an area you have visited where succession is taking place. If you can't think of an area near you, describe a place you have read about. Write down the name of the place or tell its location. Draw a picture.

Analyze Your Results

1. List evidence that succession is taking place in your area.

2. In what order will new species come to live in your area? Explain.

3. What could happen to prevent succession in your area?

For Your Reference

Science Handbook

Health Handbook

Units of Measurement

The temperature is 77 degrees Fahrenheit.

That is the same as 25 degrees Celsius.

Water boils at 212 degrees Fahrenheit.

Water freezes at 0 degrees Celsius.

I weigh 85 pounds.

That baseball bat weighs 32 ounces.

32 ounces is the same as 2 pounds.

The mass of the bat is 907 grams.

This classroom is 10 meters wide and 20 meters long.

That means the area is 200 square meters.

This bottle of juice has a volume of 1 liter.

That is a little more than 1 quart.

She can walk 20 meters in 5 seconds.

That means her speed is 4 meters per second.

Table of Measurements

International System of Units (SI)	English System of Units
Temperature	**Temperature**
Water freezes at 0°C and boils at 100°C.	Water freezes at 32°F and boils at 212°F.
Length and Distance	**Length and Distance**
1,000 meters (m) = 1 kilometer (km)	5,280 feet = 1 mile
100 centimeters (cm) = 1 meter	3 feet = 1 yard
10 millimeters (mm) = 1 centimeter	12 inches = 1 foot
Volume	**Volume of Fluids**
1,000 milliliters (mL) = 1 liter (L)	4 quarts = 1 gallon
1 cubic centimeter (cm³) = 1 milliliter	2 pints = 1 quart
	2 cups = 1 pint
Mass	8 fluid ounces = 1 cup
1,000 grams (g) = 1 kilogram (kg)	**Weight**
	2,000 pounds = 1 ton
	16 ounces = 1 pound

Use a Hand Lens

You use a hand lens to magnify an object, or make the object look larger. With a hand lens, you can see details that would be hard to see without the hand lens.

Magnify a Piece of Cereal

1. Place a piece of your favorite cereal on a flat surface. Look at the cereal carefully. Draw a picture of it.
2. Look at the cereal through the large lens of a hand lens. Move the lens toward or away from the cereal until it looks larger and in focus. Draw a picture of the cereal as you see it through the hand lens. Fill in details that you did not see before.
3. Look at the cereal through the smaller lens, which will magnify the cereal even more. If you notice more details, add them to your drawing.
4. Repeat this activity using objects you are studying in science. It might be a rock, some soil, or a seed.

Observe Seeds in a Petri Dish

Can you observe a seed as it sprouts? You can if it's in a petri dish. A petri dish is a shallow, clear, round dish with a cover.

1. Line the sides and bottom of a petri dish with a double layer of filter paper or paper towel. You may have to cut the paper to make it fit.
2. Sprinkle water on the paper to wet it.
3. Place three or four radish seeds on the wet paper in different areas of the dish. Put the lid on the dish, and keep it in a warm place.
4. Observe the seeds every day for a week. Use a hand lens to look for a tiny root pushing through the seed. Record how long it takes each seed to sprout.

Collect Data

Use a Microscope

Hand lenses make objects look several times larger. A microscope, however, can magnify an object to look hundreds of times larger.

Examine Salt Grains

1. Look at the photograph to learn the different parts of your microscope.
2. Place the microscope on a flat surface. Always carry a microscope with both hands. Hold the arm with one hand, and put your other hand beneath the base.
3. Move the mirror so that it reflects light up toward the stage. Never point the mirror directly at the Sun or a bright light. Bright light can cause permanent eye damage.
4. Place a few grains of salt on the slide. Put the slide under the stage clips. Be sure that the salt grains you are going to examine are over the hole in the stage.
5. Look through the eyepiece. Turn the focusing knob slowly until the salt grains come into focus.
6. Draw what the grains look like through the microscope.
7. Look at other objects through the microscope. Try a piece of leaf, a human hair, or a pencil mark.

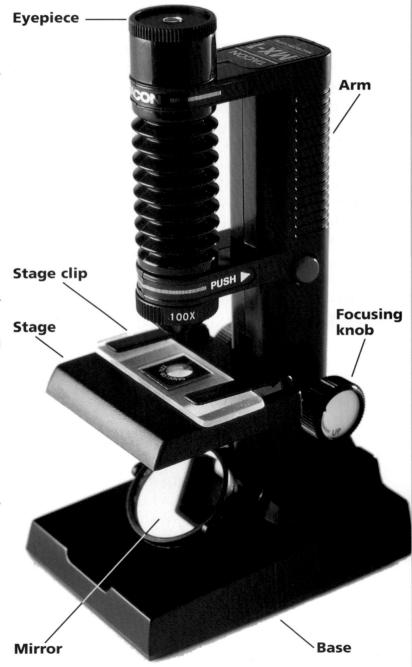

Eyepiece

Arm

Stage clip

Stage

Focusing knob

100X

PUSH ▶

Mirror

Base

Measure Time

You use timing devices to measure how long something takes to happen. Some timing devices you use in science are a clock with a second hand and a stopwatch. Which one is more accurate?

Comparing a Clock and Stopwatch

1. Look at a clock with a second hand. The second hand is the hand that you can see moving. It measures seconds.
2. Get an egg timer with falling sand or some device like a wind-up toy that runs down after a certain length of time. When the second hand of the clock points to 12, tell your partner to start the egg timer. Watch the clock while the sand in the egg timer is falling.
3. When the sand stops falling, count how many seconds it took. Record this measurement. Repeat the activity, and compare the two measurements.
4. Switch roles with your partner.
5. Look at a stopwatch. Click the button on the top right. This starts the time. Click the button again. This stops the time. Click the button on the top left. This sets the stopwatch back to zero. Notice that the stopwatch tells time in minutes, seconds, and hundredths of a second.
6. Repeat the activity in steps 1–3, using the stopwatch instead of a clock. Make sure the stopwatch is set to zero. Click the top right button to start timing the reading. Click it again when the sand stops falling. Make sure you and your partner time each other twice.

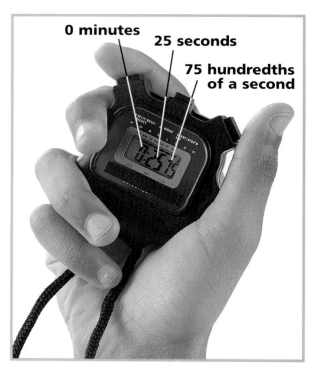

0 minutes
25 seconds
75 hundredths of a second

More About Time

1. Use the stopwatch to time how long it takes an ice cube to melt under cold running water. How long does an ice cube take to melt under warm running water?
2. Match each of these times with the action you think took that amount of time.

    a. 00:14:55
    b. 44:39:45
    c. 10:23:00

    1. Taking a shower
    2. Saying the Pledge of Allegiance
    3. Recess

Measure Length

Find Length with a Ruler

1. Look at this section of a ruler. Each centimeter is divided into 10 millimeters. How long is the paper clip?
2. The length of the paper clip is 3 centimeters plus 2 millimeters. You can write this length as 3.2 centimeters.
3. Place the ruler on your desk. Lay a pencil against the ruler so that one end of the pencil lines up with the left edge of the ruler. Record the length of the pencil.
4. Trade your pencil with a classmate. Measure and record the length of each other's pencil. Compare your answers.

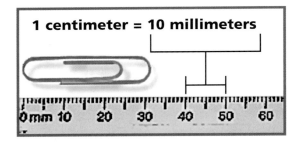

1 centimeter = 10 millimeters

Measuring Area

Area is the amount of surface something covers. To find the area of a rectangle, multiply the rectangle's length by its width. For example, the rectangle here is 3 centimeters long and 2 centimeters wide. Its area is 3 cm x 2 cm = 6 square centimeters. You write the area as 6 cm^2.

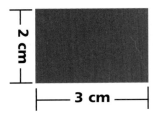

2 cm

3 cm

Opposite sides of a rectangle are parallel. The adjacent sides are perpendicular to each other (at right angles). Rectangles have symmetry. When folded in half, both halves are identical in size and shape. This is known as congruence. The two halves fit over each other exactly.

Find Length with a Meterstick

1. Line up the meterstick with the left edge of the chalkboard. Make a chalk mark on the board at the right end of the meterstick.
2. Move the meterstick so that the left edge lines up with the chalk mark. Keep the stick level. Make another mark on the board at the right end of the meterstick.
3. Continue to move the meterstick and make chalk marks until the meterstick meets or overlaps the right edge of the board.
4. Record the length of the chalkboard in centimeters by adding all the measurements you've made. Remember, a meterstick has 100 centimeters.

Estimating Length

Try estimating the length of objects in the room. Then measure the length, and compare the estimation with the measurement.

Measure Mass

Mass is the amount of matter an object has. You use a balance to measure mass. To find the mass of an object, you balance it with objects whose masses you know. Let's find the mass of a box of crayons.

Measure the Mass of a Box of Crayons

1. Place the balance on a flat, level surface. Check that the two pans are empty and clean.
2. Make sure the empty pans are balanced with each other. The pointer should point to the middle mark. If it does not, move the slider a little to the right or left to balance the pans.
3. Gently place a box of crayons on the left pan. This pan will drop lower.
4. Add masses to the right pan until the pans are balanced.
5. Add the numbers on the masses that are in the right pan. The total is the mass of the box of crayons, in grams. Record this number. After the number write a *g* for "grams."

Estimating Mass

Once you become familiar with the mass of objects, you can try estimating the masses of objects. Then you can compare the estimation with the actual mass.

More About Mass

The mass of your crayons was probably less than 100 grams. You may not have enough masses to balance a pineapple. It has a mass of about 1,000 grams. That's the same as 1 kilogram, because *kilo* means "1,000."

1. How many kilograms do all these masses add up to?
2. Which of these objects have a mass greater than 1 kilogram?

Measure Volume

Volume is the amount of space something takes up. In science you usually measure the volume of liquids by using beakers and graduated cylinders. These containers are marked in milliliters (mL).

Measure the Volume of a Liquid

1. Look at the beaker and at the graduated cylinder. The beaker has marks for each 25 mL up to 200 mL. The graduated cylinder has marks for each 1 mL up to 100 mL.
2. The surface of the water in the graduated cylinder curves up at the sides. You measure the volume by reading the height of the water at the flat part. What is the volume of water in the graduated cylinder? How much water is in the beaker? They both contain 75 mL of water.
3. Pour 50 mL of water from a pitcher into a beaker.
4. Now pour the 50 mL of water into a graduated cylinder.

Find the Volume of a Solid

Here's a way to find the volume of a solid, such as a rock.

1. Start with 50 mL of water in a graduated cylinder.
2. Place a small rock in the water. The water level rises.
3. Measure the new water level. Subtract 50 mL from the new reading. The difference is the volume of the rock. Record the volume in cm^3.

Estimating Volume

Once you become familiar with the volumes of liquids and solids, you can estimate volumes. Estimate the amount of liquid in a glass or can. Estimate the volume of an eraser.

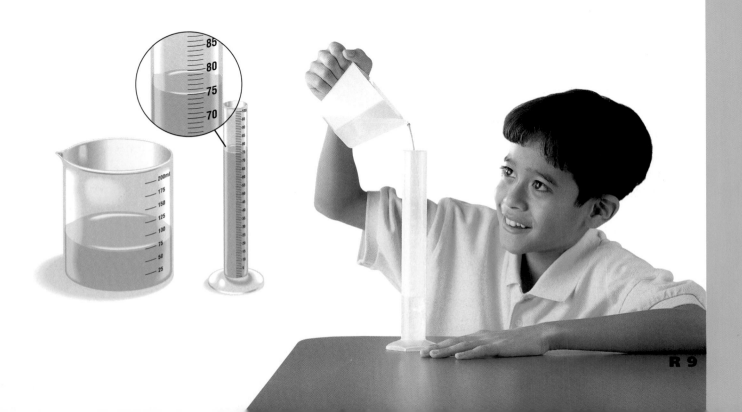

Measure Weight/Force

You use a spring scale to measure weight. An object has weight because the force of gravity pulls down on the object. Therefore, weight is a force. Weight is measured in newtons (N) like all forces.

Measure the Weight of an Object

1. Look at your spring scale to see how many newtons it measures. See how the measurements are divided. The spring scale shown here measures up to 5 N. It has a mark for every 0.1 N.
2. Hold the spring scale by the top loop. Put the object to be measured on the bottom hook. If the object will not stay on the hook, place it in a net bag. Then hang the bag from the hook.
3. Let go of the object slowly. It will pull down on a spring inside the scale. The spring is connected to a pointer. The pointer on the spring scale shown here is a small bar.
4. Wait for the pointer to stop moving. Read the number of newtons next to the pointer. This is the object's weight. The mug in the picture weighs 4 N.

More About Spring Scales

You probably weigh yourself by standing on a bathroom scale. This is a spring scale. The force of your body stretches a spring inside the scale. The dial on the scale is probably marked in pounds—the English unit of weight. One pound is equal to about 4.5 newtons.

A bathroom scale, a grocery scale, and a kitchen scale are some other spring scales you may have seen.

Measure Temperature

You use a thermometer to measure temperature—how hot or cold something is. A thermometer is made of a thin tube with colored liquid inside. When the liquid gets warmer, it expands and moves up the tube. When the liquid gets cooler, it contracts and moves down the tube. You may have seen most temperatures measured in degrees Fahrenheit (°F). Scientists measure temperature in degrees Celsius (°C).

°F   °C

Water boils

Water freezes

Room temperature

Read a Thermometer

1. Look at the thermometer shown here. It has two scales—a Fahrenheit scale and a Celsius scale.
2. What is the temperature shown on the thermometer? At what temperature does water freeze?

What Is Convection?

1. Fill a large beaker about two-thirds full of cool water. Find the temperature of the water by holding a thermometer in the water. Do not let the bulb at the bottom of the thermometer touch the sides or bottom of the beaker.
2. Keep the thermometer in the water until the liquid in the tube stops moving—about 1 minute. Read and record the temperature in °C.
3. Sprinkle a little fish food on the surface of the water in the beaker. Do

not knock the beaker, and most of the food will stay on top.

4. Carefully place the beaker on a hot plate. A hot plate is a small electric stove. Plug in the hot plate, and turn the control knob to a middle setting.
5. After 1 minute measure the temperature of water near the bottom of the beaker. At the same time, a classmate should measure the temperature of water near the top of the beaker. Record these temperatures. Is water near the bottom of the beaker heating up faster than near the top?
6. As the water heats up, notice what happens to the fish food. How do you know that warmer water at the bottom of the beaker rises and cooler water at the top sinks?

11

Use Calculators

Sometimes after you make measurements, you have to analyze your data to see what it means. This might involve doing calculations with your data. A calculator helps you do time-consuming calculations.

Find an Average

After you collect a set of measurements, you may want to get an idea of a typical measurement in that set. What if, for example, you are doing a weather project? As part of the project, you are studying rainfall data of a nearby town. The table shows how much rain fell in that town each week during the summer.

Week	Rain (cm)
1	2.0
2	1.4
3	0.0
4	0.5
5	1.2
6	2.5
7	1.8
8	1.4
9	2.4
10	8.6
11	7.5

What if you want to get an idea of how much rain fell during a typical week in the summer? In other words, you want to find the average for the set of data. There are three kinds of averages—mean, median, and mode. Does it matter which one you use?

Find the Mean

The mean is what most people think of when they hear the word *average*. You can use a calculator to find the mean.

1. Make sure the calculator is on.
2. Add the numbers. To add a series of numbers, enter the first number and press ⊕. Repeat until you enter the last number. See the hints below. After your last number, press ⊟. Your total should be 29.3.
3. While entering so many numbers, it's easy to make a mistake and hit the wrong key. If you make a mistake, correct it by pressing the clear entry key, CE. Then continue entering the rest of the numbers.
4. Find the mean by dividing your total by the number of weeks. If 29.3 is displayed, press ⊘ ① ① ⊟. Rounded up to one decimal point, your mean should be 2.7.

Hints:
- If the only number to the right of the decimal point is 0, you don't have to enter it into the calculator. To enter 2.0, just press ②.
- If the only number to the left of the decimal point is 0, you don't have to enter it into the calculator. To enter 0.5, just press ·⑤.

Use Technology

Find the Median

The median is the middle number when the numbers are arranged in order of size. When the rainfall measurements are arranged in order of size, they look like this.

0.0	
0.5	
1.2	
1.4	The median is 1.8.
1.4	This number is in
1.8 ————	the middle; there
2.0	are five numbers
2.4	above it and five
2.5	numbers below it.
7.5	
8.6	

Find the Mode

The mode is the number that occurs most frequently. From the ranked set of data above, you can see that the most frequent number is 1.4. It occurs twice. Here are your three different averages from the same set of data.

Average Weekly Rainfall (cm)

Mean	2.7
Median	1.8
Mode	1.4

Why is the mean so much higher than the median or mode? The mean is affected greatly by the last two weeks when it rained a lot. A typical week for that summer was much drier than either of those last two weeks. The median or mode gives a better idea of rainfall for a typical week.

Find the Percent

Sometimes numbers are given as percents (%). *Percent* literally means "per hundred." For example, 28% means 28 out of 100. What if there are about 14,000 trees in the forest and 28% are over 50 years old? How many of them are over 50 years old? Use your calculator. You want to find 28% of 14,000. Press [1][4][0][0][0] [×] [2][8][%]. The answer should be 3,920.

Mathematical Operations

Addition and subtraction are reverse operations, or inverses of each other. For example:

$$2 + 3 = 5;$$
$$5 - 3 = 2;$$
$$5 - 2 = 3.$$

Similarly, multiplication and division are also inverses of each other. For example:

$$6 \times 3 = 18;$$
$$18 \div 6 = 3;$$
$$18 \div 3 = 6.$$

Mathematical Statements

Mathematical statements using symbols may be true only when the symbols are replaced by certain numbers. For example:

$$A < B$$

If $A = 2$ and $B = 3$, the statement is true. If $A = 3$ and $B = 2$, the statement is false.

Use Computers

A computer has many uses. The Internet connects your computer to many other computers around the world, so you can collect all kinds of information. You can use a computer to show this information and write reports. Best of all you can use a computer to explore, discover, and learn.

You can also get information from CD-ROMs. They are computer disks that can hold large amounts of information. You can fit a whole encyclopedia on one CD-ROM.

Use Computers for a Project

Here is how one group of students uses computers as they work on a weather project.

1. The students use instruments to measure temperature, wind speed, wind direction, and other parts of the weather. They input this information, or data, into the computer. The students keep the data in a table. This helps them compare the data from one day to the next.

2. The teacher finds out that another group of students in a town 200 kilometers to the west is also doing a weather project. The two groups use the Internet to talk to each other and share data. When a storm happens in the town to the west, that group tells the other group that it's coming their way.

3. The students want to find out more. They decide to stay on the Internet and send questions to a local TV weather forecaster. She has a Web site and answers questions from students every day.

4. Meanwhile some students go to the library to gather more information from a CD-ROM. The CD-ROM has an encyclopedia that includes movie clips. The clips give examples of different kinds of storms.

5. The students have kept all their information in a folder called Weather Project. Now they use that information to write a report about the weather. On the computer they can move around paragraphs, add words, take out words, put in diagrams, and draw weather maps. Then they print the report in color.

Make Graphs to Organize Data

When you do an experiment in science, you collect information. To find out what your information means, you can organize it into graphs. There are many kinds of graphs.

Bar Graphs

A bar graph uses bars to show information. For example, what if you do an experiment by wrapping wire around a nail and connecting the ends of the wire to a battery? The nail then becomes a magnet that can pick up paper clips. The graph shows that the more you wrap the wire around the nail, the more paper clips it picks up. How many paper clips did the nail with 20 coils pick up? With 50 coils?

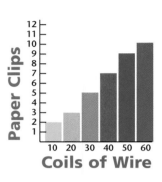

Pictographs

A pictograph uses symbols, or pictures, to show information. What if you collect information about how much water your family uses each day? The table shows what you find.

You can organize this information into the pictograph shown here. The pictograph has to explain what the symbol on the graph means. In this case each bottle means 20 liters of water. A half bottle means half of 20, or 10 liters of water.

1. Which activity uses the most water?
2. Which activity uses the least water?

Activity	Water Used Each Day (L)
Drinking	10
Showering	180
Bathing	240
Brushing teeth	80
Washing dishes	140
Washing hands	30
Washing clothes	280
Flushing toilet	90

A Family's Daily Use of Water

Drinking	
Showering	
Bathing	🛢 = 20 liters of water
Brushing teeth	
Washing dishes	
Washing hands	
Washing clothes	
Flushing toilet	

Represent Data

Circle Graphs

A circle graph is helpful to show how a complete set of data is divided into parts. The circle graph here shows how water is used in the United States. What is the single largest use of water?

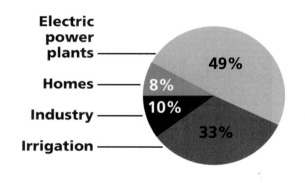

Electric power plants — 49%
Homes — 8%
Industry — 10%
Irrigation — 33%

Line Graphs

A line graph shows information by connecting dots plotted on the graph. It shows change over time. For example, what if you measure the temperature out of doors every hour starting at 6 A.M.? The table shows what you find.

Time	Temperature (°C)
6 A.M.	10
7 A.M.	12
8 A.M.	14
9 A.M.	16
10 A.M.	18
11 A.M.	20

You can organize this information into a line graph. Follow these steps.

1. Make a scale along the bottom and side of the graph. The scales should include all the numbers in the chart. Label the scales.
2. Plot points on the graph. For example, place your finger at the "6 A.M." on the bottom line. Place a finger from your other hand on the "10" on the left line. Move your "6 A.M." finger up and your "10" finger to the right until they meet, and make a pencil point. Plot the other points in this way.
3. Connect the points with a line.

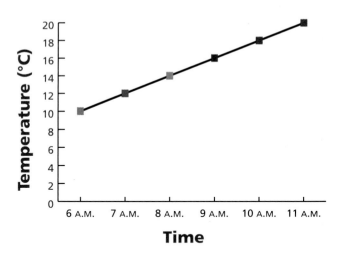

The line graph to the right organizes measurements you collected so that you can easily compare them.

1. Between which two weeks did the plant grow most?
2. When did plant growth begin to level off?

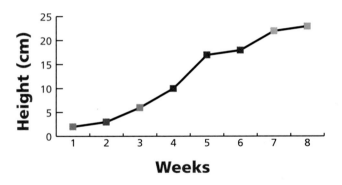

Make Maps to Show Information

Locate Places

A map is a drawing that shows an area from above. Most maps have coordinates—numbers and letters along the top and side. Coordinates help you find places easily. For example, what if you wanted to find the library on the map? It is located at B4. Place a finger on the letter B along the side of the map, and another finger on the number 4 at the top. Then move your fingers straight across and down the map until they meet. The library is located where the coordinates B and 4 meet, or very nearby.

1. What color building is located at F6?
2. The hospital is located three blocks north and two blocks east of the library. What are its coordinates?
3. Make a map of an area in your community. It might be a park or the area between your home and school. Include coordinates. Use a compass to find north, and mark north on your map. Exchange maps with class-mates, and answer each other's questions.

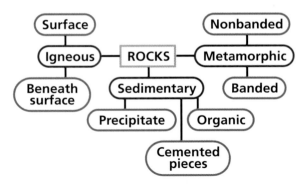

Idea Maps

The map below shows how places are connected to each other. Idea maps, on the other hand, show how ideas are connected to each other. Idea maps help you organize information about a topic.

The idea map above connects ideas about rocks. This map shows that there are three major types of rock—igneous, sedimentary, and metamorphic. Connections to each rock type provide further information. For example, this map reminds you that igneous rocks are classified into those that form at Earth's surface and far beneath it.

Make an idea map about a topic you are learning in science. Your map can include words, phrases, or even sentences. Arrange your map in a way that makes sense to you and helps you understand the ideas.

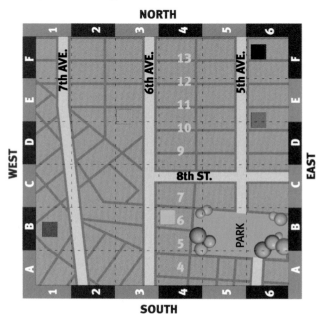

Make Tables and Charts to Organize Information

Tables help you organize data during experiments. Most tables have columns that run up and down, and rows that run across. The columns and rows have headings that tell you what kind of data goes in each part of the table.

A Sample Table

What if you are going to do an experiment to find out how long different kinds of seeds take to sprout? Before you begin the experiment, you should set up your table. Follow these steps.

1. In this experiment you will plant 20 radish seeds, 20 bean seeds, and 20 corn seeds. Your table must show how many radish seeds, bean seeds, and corn seeds sprouted on days 1, 2, 3, 4, and 5.

2. Make your table with columns, rows, and headings. You might use a computer to make a table. Some computer programs let you build a table with just the click of a mouse. You can delete or add columns and rows if you need to.

3. Give your table a title. Your table could look like the one here.

Make a Table

Now what if you are going to do an experiment to find out how temperature affects the sprouting of seeds? You will plant 20 bean seeds in each of two trays. You will keep each tray at a different temperature, as shown below, and observe the trays for seven days. Make a table you can use for this experiment.

Make a Chart

A chart is simply a table with pictures as well as words to label the rows or columns.

The Human Body

Like all organisms, humans are made up of cells. In fact, the human body is made of trillions of cells. These cells are organized into tissues, a group of similar cells that perform a specific function. Tissues, in turn, form organs. Your heart and lungs are examples of organs. Finally, organs work together as part of organ systems. Your heart, for example, is part of the circulatory system.

Levels of Organization

- Cells
- Tissues
- Organs
- Organ Systems
- Organism

Including the skin, or integumentary system, the human body has 11 major organ systems. These body systems each have specific functions, and they also work together as parts of the human body as a whole.

Human Body Systems	
System	**Function**
Nervous System	control
Skeletal System	support
Integumentary System	protection
Muscular System	movement
Circulatory System	transport
Respiratory System	oxygen/ carbon dioxide exchange
Digestive System	food absorption
Excretory System	waste removal
Endocrine System	regulation and control
Reproductive System	reproduction
Immune System	protection

The Nervous System

The nervous system has two parts. The brain and the spinal cord are the central nervous system. All other nerves are the outer, or peripheral, nervous system.

The largest part of the brain is the cerebrum. A deep groove separates the right half, or hemisphere, of the cerebrum from the left half. Both the right and left hemispheres of the cerebrum contain control centers for the senses.

The cerebellum lies below the cerebrum. It coordinates the skeletal muscles so they work smoothly together. It also helps in keeping balance.

The brain stem connects to the spinal cord. The lowest part of the brain stem is the medulla. It controls heartbeat, breathing, blood pressure, and the muscles in the digestive system.

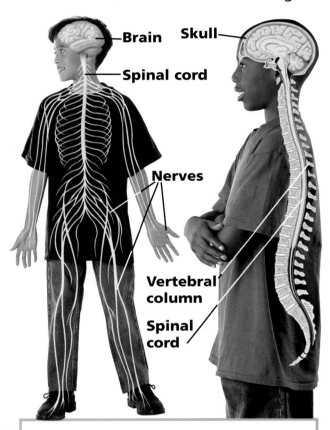

Brain · Skull · Spinal cord · Nerves · Vertebral column · Spinal cord

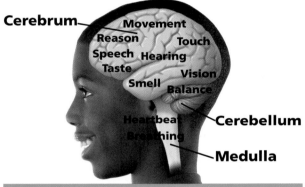

Cerebrum · Movement · Reason · Touch · Speech · Hearing · Taste · Vision · Smell · Balance · Heartbeat · Breathing · Cerebellum · Medulla

Parts of a Neuron

The nerves in the nervous system are made up of nerve cells called *neurons.* Each neuron has three main parts—a cell body, dendrites, and an axon. Dendrites are branching nerve fibers that carry impulses, or electrical signals, toward the cell body. An axon is a nerve fiber that carries impulses away from the cell body.

When an impulse reaches the tip of an axon, it must cross a tiny gap to reach the next neuron. This gap between neurons is called a *synapse.*

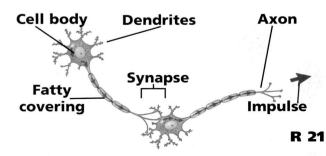

Cell body · Dendrites · Axon · Synapse · Fatty covering · Impulse

CARE!

- Wear protective headgear when you play sports or exercise.

- Stay away from drugs, such as stimulants, which can speed up the nervous system.

- Stay away from alcohol, which is a depressant and slows down the nervous system.

The Senses

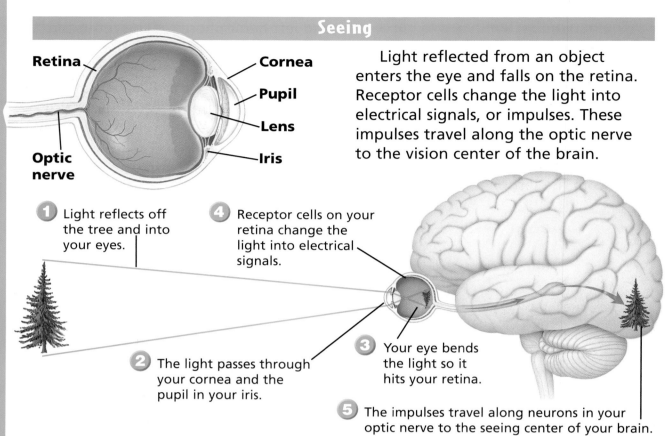

Retina **Cornea**
Pupil
Lens
Optic nerve **Iris**

Light reflected from an object enters the eye and falls on the retina. Receptor cells change the light into electrical signals, or impulses. These impulses travel along the optic nerve to the vision center of the brain.

1 Light reflects off the tree and into your eyes.

4 Receptor cells on your retina change the light into electrical signals.

2 The light passes through your cornea and the pupil in your iris.

3 Your eye bends the light so it hits your retina.

5 The impulses travel along neurons in your optic nerve to the seeing center of your brain.

Hearing

Sound waves enter the ear and cause the eardrum to vibrate. Receptor cells in the ear change the sound waves into impulses that travel along the auditory nerve to the hearing center of the brain.

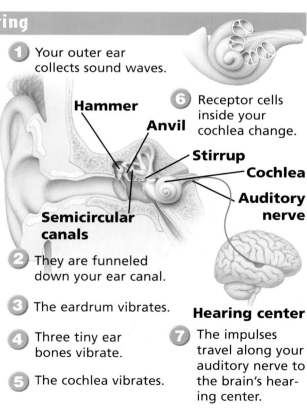

1 Your outer ear collects sound waves.

6 Receptor cells inside your cochlea change.

Hammer
Anvil
Stirrup
Cochlea
Auditory nerve
Semicircular canals

2 They are funneled down your ear canal.

3 The eardrum vibrates.

4 Three tiny ear bones vibrate.

5 The cochlea vibrates.

Hearing center

7 The impulses travel along your auditory nerve to the brain's hearing center.

CARE!

- To avoid straining your eye muscles, don't sit too close to the TV screen or computer monitor.

- Avoid loud music. Turn down the volume when wearing headphones.

The Senses

Smelling

The sense of smell is really the ability to detect chemicals in the air. When a person breathes, chemicals dissolve in mucus in the upper part of the nose. When the chemicals come in contact with receptor cells, the cells send impulses along the olfactory nerve to the smelling center of the brain.

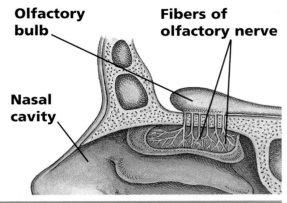

Olfactory bulb

Fibers of olfactory nerve

Nasal cavity

Tasting

When a person eats, chemicals in food dissolve in saliva. Saliva carries the chemicals to taste buds on the tongue. Inside each taste bud are receptors that can sense the four main tastes—sweet, sour, salty, and bitter. The receptors send impulses along a nerve to the taste center of the brain. The brain identifies the taste of the food, which is usually a combination of the four main tastes.

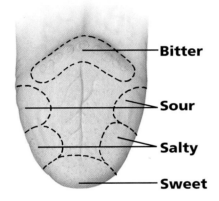

Bitter

Sour

Salty

Sweet

Touching

Receptor cells in the skin help a person tell hot from cold, wet from dry, and the light touch of a feather from the pressure of stepping on a stone. Each receptor cell sends impulses along sensory nerves to the spinal cord. The spinal cord then sends the impulses to the touch center of the brain.

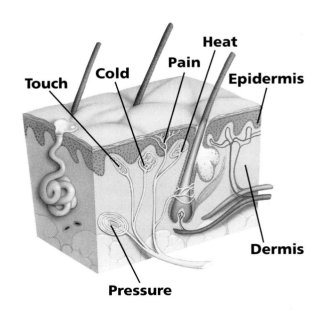

Touch

Cold

Pain

Heat

Epidermis

Dermis

Pressure

CARE!

- To prevent the spread of germs, always cover your mouth and nose when you cough or sneeze.

The Skeletal System

The body has a supporting frame, called a skeleton, which is made up of bones. The skeleton has several jobs.

- It gives the body its shape.
- It protects organs in the body.
- It works with muscles to move the body.

Each of the 206 bones of the skeleton is the size and shape best fitted to do its job. For example, long and strong leg bones support the body's weight.

CARE!

- ● Exercise to keep your skeletal system in good shape.

- ● Don't overextend your joints.

- ● Eat foods rich in vitamins and minerals. Your bones need the minerals, calcium, and phosphorus to grow strong.

The Integumentary System

The skeleton and the organ systems are covered by an outer layer of skin. The skin is the largest organ of the human body. It is part of the integumentary system. Other parts of the integumentary system are your hair, nails, and glands in the skin. The skin has several functions.

- It protects your internal organs.
- It protects your body from injury and infection.
- It helps regulate body temperature.
- It helps remove wastes.

The Skeleton

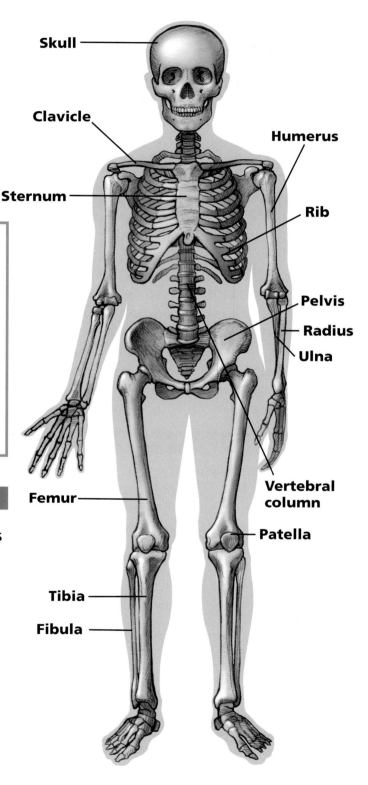

- Skull
- Clavicle
- Humerus
- Sternum
- Rib
- Pelvis
- Radius
- Ulna
- Vertebral column
- Femur
- Patella
- Tibia
- Fibula

Joints

The skeleton has different types of joints. A joint is a place where two or more bones meet. Joints can be classified into three major groups—immovable joints, partly movable joints, and movable joints.

Types of Joints

Immovable Joints

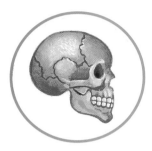

Head

Immovable joints are places where bones fit together too tightly to move. Nearly all the 29 bones in the skull meet at immovable joints. Only the lower jaw can move.

Partly Movable Joints

Partly movable joints are places where bones can move only a little. Ribs are connected to the sternum, or breastbone, with these joints.

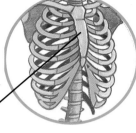

Sternum

Ribs

Movable Joints

Movable joints are places where bones can move easily.

Gliding joint

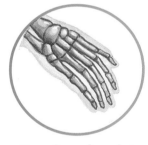

Hand and wrist

Small bones in the wrists and ankles meet at gliding joints. The bones can slide against one another. These joints allow some movement in all directions.

Ball-and-socket joint

The hips are examples of ball-and-socket joints. The ball of one bone fits into the socket, or cup, of another bone. These joints allow bones to move back and forth, in a circle, and side to side.

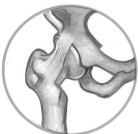

Hip

Hinge joint

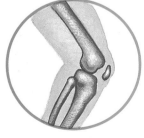

Knee

The knees are hinge joints. A hinge joint is similar to a door hinge. It allows bones to move back and forth in one direction.

Pivot joint

The joint between the skull and neck is a pivot joint. It allows the head to move up and down, and side to side.

Neck

The Muscular System

Three types of muscles make up the body—skeletal muscle, cardiac muscle, and smooth muscle.

The muscles that are attached to and move bones are called *skeletal muscles.* These muscles are attached to bones by a tough cord called a *tendon.* Skeletal muscles pull bones to move them. Muscles do not push bones.

Cardiac muscles are found in only one place in the body—the heart. The walls of the heart are made of strong cardiac muscles. When cardiac muscles contract, they squeeze blood out of the heart. When cardiac muscles relax, the heart fills with more blood.

Smooth muscles make up internal organs and blood vessels. Smooth muscles in the lungs help a person breathe. Those in the blood vessels help control blood flow around the body.

CARE!

- **Exercise to strengthen your muscles.**
- **Eat the right foods.**
- **Get plenty of rest.**
- **Never take steroids unless your doctor tells you to.**

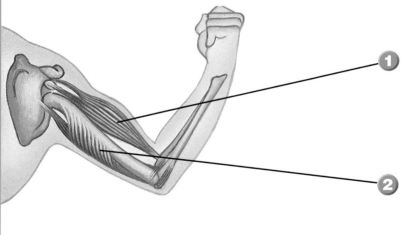

1 A message from you brain causes this muscle, called the biceps (BIGH·seps), to contract. When a muscle contracts, it becomes shorter and thicker. As the biceps contacts, it pulls on the arm bone it is attached to.

2 Most muscles work in pairs to move bones. This muscle, called the triceps (TRIGH·seps), relaxes when the biceps contacts. When a muscle relaxes, it becomes longer and thinner.

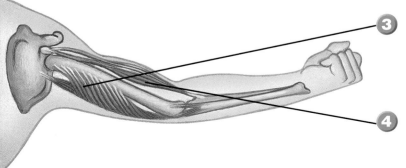

3 To straighten your arm, a message from your brain causes the triceps to contract. When the triceps contracts, it pulls on the bone it is attached to.

4 As the triceps contracts, the biceps relaxes. Your arm straightens.

Stimulus and Response

The nervous system, the skeletal system, and the muscular system work together to help you adjust to your surroundings. Anything in the environment that requires your body to adjust is called a *stimulus* (plural: stimuli). A reaction to a stimulus is called a *response*.

As you learned, nerve cells are called *neurons.* There are three kinds of neurons: sensory, associative, and motor. Each kind does a different job to help your body respond to stimuli.

- The job of your sensory neurons is to collect information from stimuli and send it to your brain and spinal cord. When you touch a sharp tack, sensory neurons alert your brain. The sensory neurons carry the message that your finger has touched a tack (stimulus) to the associative neurons in the brain and spinal cord.

- Associative neurons pass impulses from sensory to motor neurons. The message is interpreted and sent to the motor neurons.

- Motor neurons carry impulses from your brain and spinal cord to your muscles. The motor neurons cause your finger to move away from the tack (response).

In addition to responding to external stimuli, your body also responds to internal changes. Your body regulates its internal environment to maintain a stable condition for survival. This is called a *steady-state* condition.

Nerve Response

Nerves respond to a sharp object.

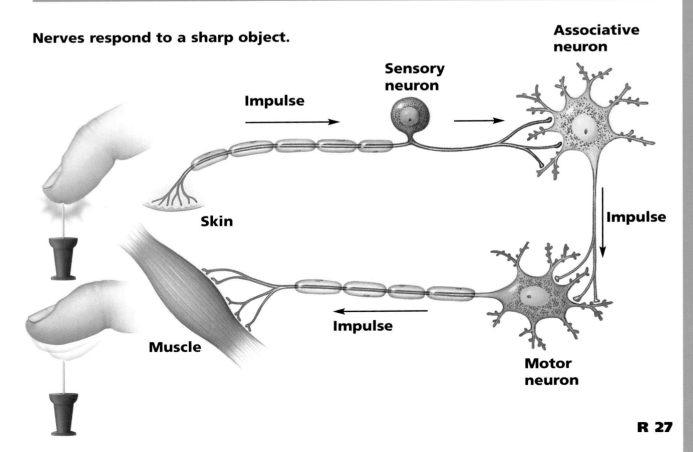

Impulse · Skin · Sensory neuron · Associative neuron · Impulse · Motor neuron · Impulse · Muscle

The Circulatory System

The circulatory system consists of the heart, blood vessels, and blood. Circulation is the flow of blood through the body. Blood is a liquid that contains red blood cells, white blood cells, and platelets. Red blood cells carry oxygen and nutrients to cells. White blood cells work to fight germs that enter the body. Platelets are cell fragments that make the blood clot.

The heart is a muscular organ about the size of a fist. It beats about 70 to 90 times a minute, pumping blood through the blood vessels. Arteries carry blood away from the heart. Some arteries carry blood to the lungs, where the cells pick up oxygen. Other arteries carry oxygen-rich blood from the lungs to all other parts of the body. Veins carry blood from other parts of the body back to the heart. Blood in most veins carries the wastes released by cells and has little oxygen. Blood flows from arteries to veins through narrow vessels called capillaries.

Pulse Rate and Pulse Points

You can tell how fast your heart is beating by checking your *pulse rate*. Take your pulse by putting the first and second fingers of one hand on the inside of the wrist of the other hand, just below the thumb. What you feel is the blood being pumped by your heart through arteries that lie close to the surface of the skin. Count the number of times you feel your heart pump in one minute. This is your pulse rate.

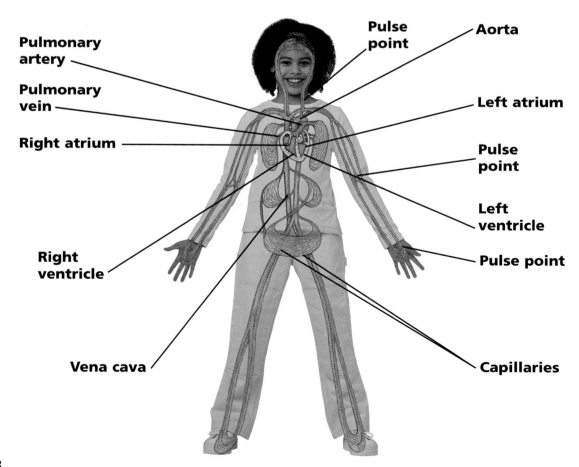

Pulmonary artery

Pulmonary vein

Right atrium

Right ventricle

Vena cava

Pulse point

Aorta

Left atrium

Pulse point

Left ventricle

Pulse point

Capillaries

The Heart

The heart has two sides, right and left, separated by a thick muscular wall. Each side has two chambers for blood. The upper chamber is the atrium. The lower chamber is the ventricle. Blood enters the heart through the vena cava. It leaves the heart through the aorta.

The pulmonary artery carries blood from the body into the lungs. Here carbon dioxide leaves the blood to be exhaled by the lungs. Fresh oxygen enters the blood to be carried to every cell in the body. Blood returns from the lungs to the heart through the pulmonary veins.

CARE!

- **Don't smoke. The nicotine in tobacco makes the heart beat faster and work harder to pump blood.**

- **Never take illegal drugs, such as cocaine or heroin. They can damage the heart and cause heart failure.**

How the Heart Works

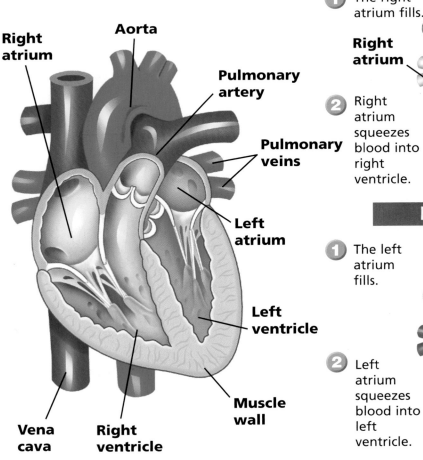

Right atrium

Aorta

Pulmonary artery

Pulmonary veins

Left atrium

Left ventricle

Muscle wall

Vena cava

Right ventricle

To the Lungs

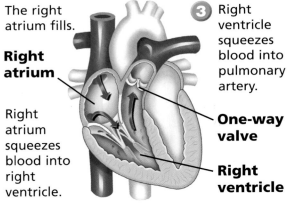

1. The right atrium fills.

Right atrium

2. Right atrium squeezes blood into right ventricle.

3. Right ventricle squeezes blood into pulmonary artery.

One-way valve

Right ventricle

From the Lungs

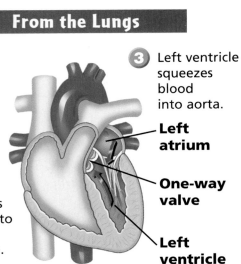

1. The left atrium fills.

2. Left atrium squeezes blood into left ventricle.

3. Left ventricle squeezes blood into aorta.

Left atrium

One-way valve

Left ventricle

The Respiratory System

The process of getting and using oxygen in the body is called respiration. When a person inhales, air is pulled into the nose or mouth. The air travels down into the trachea. In the chest the trachea divides into two bronchial tubes. One bronchial tube enters each lung. Each bronchial tube branches into smaller tubes called bronchioles.

At the end of each bronchiole are tiny air sacs called alveoli. The alveoli exchange carbon dioxide for oxygen.

Oxygen comes from the air a person breathes. Two main muscles control breathing. One is located between the ribs. The other is a dome-shaped sheet of muscle called the diaphragm.

To inhale, the diaphragm contracts and pulls down. Other muscles pull the ribs up and out. This makes more room in the chest. Air rushes into the lungs and fills the space.

To exhale, the diaphragm relaxes and returns to its dome shape. The lungs get smaller and force the air out.

CARE!

- **Don't smoke. Smoking damages your respiratory system.**
- **Exercise to strengthen your breathing muscles.**
- **If you ever have trouble breathing, tell an adult at once.**

1 Carbon dioxide diffuses into the alveoli. From there it is exhaled.

2 Fresh oxygen diffuses from the alveoli to the blood.

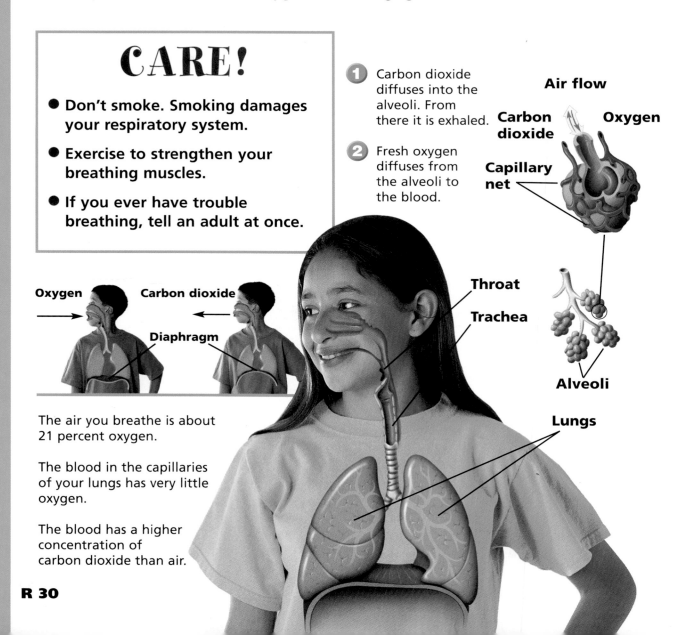

Air flow

Carbon dioxide   **Oxygen**

Capillary net

Throat

Trachea

Alveoli

Lungs

Oxygen   Carbon dioxide

Diaphragm

The air you breathe is about 21 percent oxygen.

The blood in the capillaries of your lungs has very little oxygen.

The blood has a higher concentration of carbon dioxide than air.

Effects of Exercise

Any type of exercise uses your muscles. When you exercise, your muscles need three things:

- They need oxygen.
- They need to remove wastes.
- They need to get rid of heat.

When you exercise, several things happen to your body. Your heart beats faster, you breathe heavier and faster, and you sweat.

If you are going to be exercising for more than a couple of minutes, your body needs to get oxygen to the muscles or the muscles will stop working. Your body increases the flow of oxygen-rich blood to working muscle as follows:

- Your rate and depth of breathing increase to take in more oxygen.
- Your heart beats faster so that it can pump more oxygen-rich blood to the muscles.

Sweating helps remove both wastes and heat that result from exercise.

The Digestive System

Digestion is the process of breaking down food into simple substances the body can use. Digestion begins when a person chews food. Chewing breaks the food down into smaller pieces and moistens it with saliva. Saliva is produced by the salivary glands.

Digested food is absorbed in the small intestine. The walls of the small intestine are lined with villi. Villi are tiny fingerlike projections that absorb digested food. From the villi the blood transports nutrients to every part of the body.

The shape of the small intestine's villi increases the amount of nutrients that can be absorbed from the food.

CARE!

- Chew your food well.

- Drink plenty of water to help move food through your digestive system.

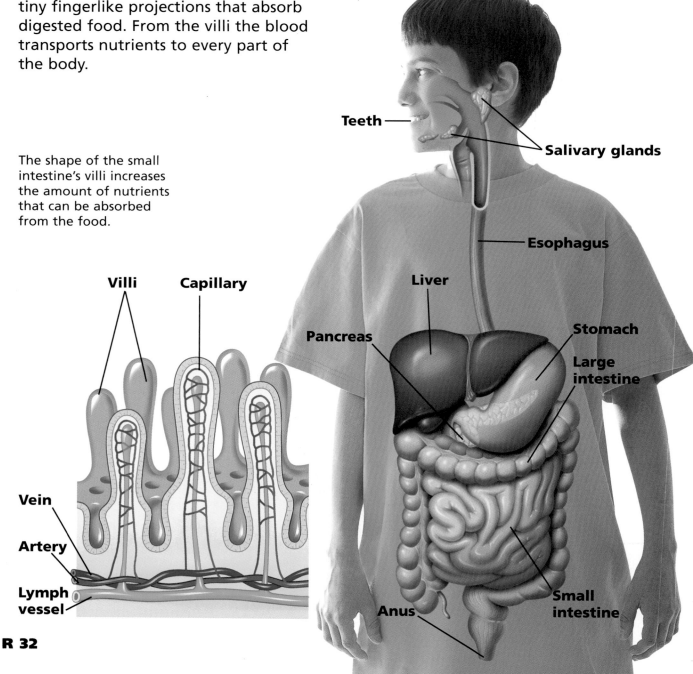

Villi

Capillary

Vein

Artery

Lymph vessel

Teeth

Salivary glands

Esophagus

Liver

Pancreas

Stomach

Large intestine

Small intestine

Anus

The Digestive System

Mechanical and Chemical Digestion

Digestion is both mechanical and chemical. Chewing is the first step in digestion. Chewing is *mechanical digestion*, the physical process of breaking food down into smaller pieces. As you chew, saliva begins to break the food into simpler molecules. This is *chemical digestion*.

After you swallow your food, both mechanical and chemical digestion continue in the stomach. Stomach muscles churn food particles into smaller pieces. Glands lining the stomach produce strong digestive juices.

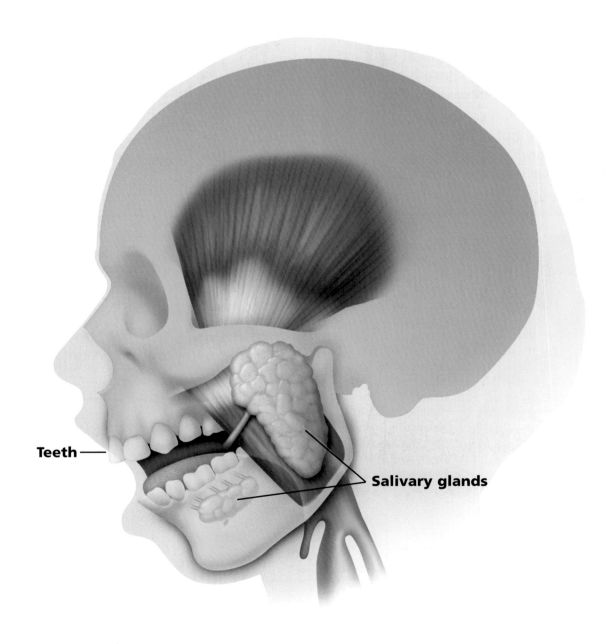

Teeth

Salivary glands

The Excretory System

Excretion is the process of removing waste products from the body. The liver filters wastes from the blood and converts them into urea. Urea is then carried to the kidneys for excretion. Each kidney contains more than a million nephrons. Nephrons are structures in the kidneys that filter blood.

The skin takes part in excretion when a person sweats. Glands in the inner layer of the skin produce sweat. Sweat is mostly water. Sweat tastes salty because it contains mineral salts the body doesn't need. There is also a tiny amount of urea in sweat.

Sweat is excreted by the sweat glands onto the outer layer of the skin. There it evaporates into the air. Evaporation takes place in part because of body heat. When sweat evaporates, a person feels cooler. On hot days or when exercising, a person sweats more to keep the body from overheating.

How You Sweat

Glands under your skin push sweat up to the surface, where it collects.

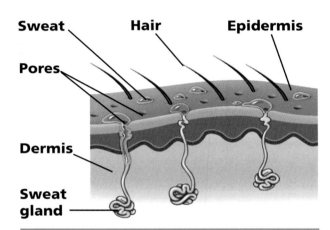

Sweat · Hair · Epidermis · Pores · Dermis · Sweat gland

How Your Kidneys Work

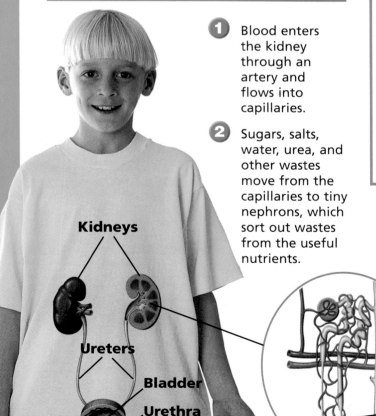

Kidneys · Ureters · Bladder · Urethra

1. Blood enters the kidney through an artery and flows into capillaries.

2. Sugars, salts, water, urea, and other wastes move from the capillaries to tiny nephrons, which sort out wastes from the useful nutrients.

CARE!

- **Drink plenty of water to help the kidneys do their job and to replace water loss from sweating.**

- **Wash regularly to avoid body odor, clogged pores, and skin irritation.**

3. The nutrients return to the blood and flow back out through veins.

4. Urea and other wastes become urine, which flows down the ureters.

5. Urine is stored in the bladder and excreted through the urethra.

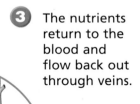

Artery · Vein · Capillaries

The Excretory System

Removing Excess Heat

In addition to waste removal, one of the skin's most important jobs is to maintain internal body temperature. The skin does this by removing excess heat. Two things happen when you exercise: your face gets red and you sweat. Both are ways of getting rid of excess heat.

The nervous system, the circulatory system, and the skin all work together to regulate body temperature. The diagram below shows what happens when your body heats up as a result of exercise.

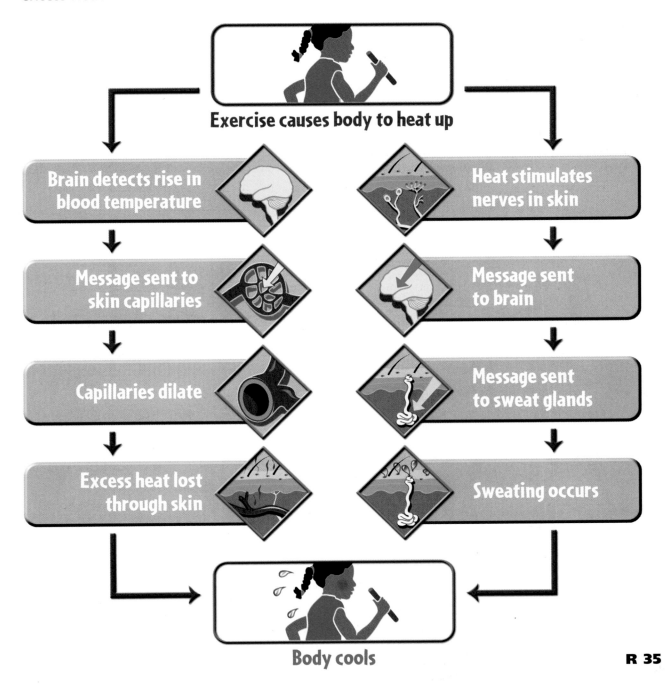

Exercise causes body to heat up

Brain detects rise in blood temperature	Heat stimulates nerves in skin
Message sent to skin capillaries	Message sent to brain
Capillaries dilate	Message sent to sweat glands
Excess heat lost through skin	Sweating occurs

Body cools

The Endocrine System

Hormones are chemicals that control body functions. A gland that produces hormones is called an endocrine gland. Sweat from sweat glands flows out of tubes called ducts. Endocrine glands have no ducts.

The endocrine glands are scattered around the body. Each gland makes one or more hormones. Every hormone seeks out a target organ, the place in the body where the hormone acts.

The endocrine glands help to maintain a *steady-state* condition in your body. They can turn the production of hormones on or off when they sense that too little or too much is being produced.

CARE!

- Doctors can treat many diseases, such as diabetes, caused by endocrine glands that produce too little or too much of a hormone.

Some Glands in the Endocrine System

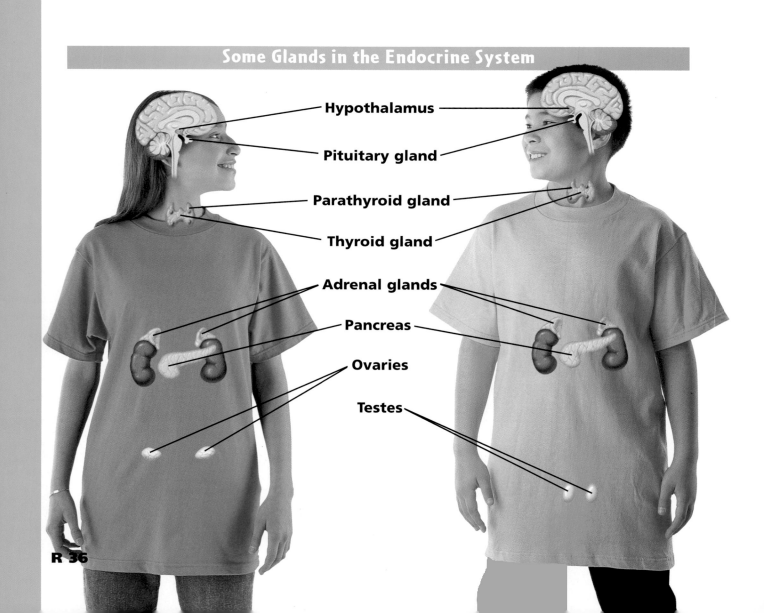

Hypothalamus

Pituitary gland

Parathyroid gland

Thyroid gland

Adrenal glands

Pancreas

Ovaries

Testes

The Reproductive System

The testes are the male reproductive organs. At puberty the testes begin to produce sperm. Sperm move through sperm ducts, where they mix with fluid from endocrine glands.

The ovaries are the female reproductive organs, which contain eggs. After puberty one mature egg is released about once every 28 days. The egg moves to the oviduct, a narrow tube leading from the ovary.

CARE!

- Abstinence is the only sure way to avoid sexually transmitted diseases.

The Male Reproductive System

Sperm move from the testes through sperm ducts, where they mix with fluid from the glands. The sperm and fluid move through the urethra.

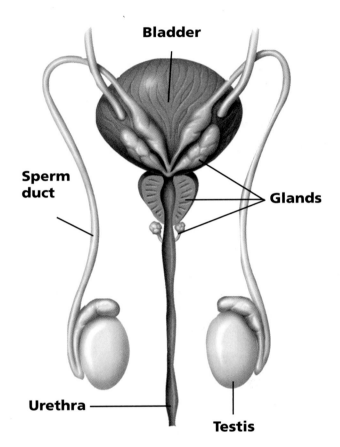

Bladder

Sperm duct

Glands

Urethra

Testis

The Female Reproductive System

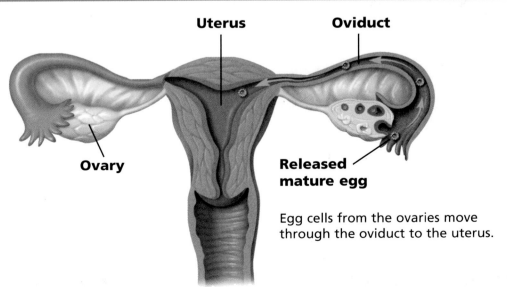

Uterus

Oviduct

Ovary

Released mature egg

Egg cells from the ovaries move through the oviduct to the uterus.

The Immune System

The immune system helps the body fight disease. Inside some bones is a soft tissue known as red marrow that fills the spaces in spongy bone. Red marrow makes new red blood cells, platelets that stop a cut from bleeding, and germ-fighting white blood cells.

There are white blood cells in the blood vessels and in the lymph vessels. Lymph vessels are similar to blood vessels. Instead of blood, they carry lymph. Lymph is a straw-colored fluid surrounding body cells.

Lymph nodes filter out harmful materials in lymph. Like red marrow, they also produce white blood cells to fight infections. Swollen lymph nodes in the neck are a clue that the body is fighting germs.

CARE!

● **Be sure to get immunized against common diseases.**

● **Keep cuts clean to prevent infection.**

1 A bone is covered with a tough but thin membrane that has many small blood vessels. The blood vessels bring nutrients and oxygen to the living parts of the bone and remove wastes.

2 Inside some bones is a soft tissue known as marrow. Yellow marrow is made mostly of fat cells and is one of the body's energy reserves. It is usually found in the long, hollow spaces of long bones.

3 Part of the bone is compact, or solid. It is made up of living bone cells and nonliving materials. The nonliving part is made up of layers of hardened minerals such as calcium and phosphorus. In between the mineral layers are living bone cells.

4 Red marrow fills the spaces in spongy bone. Red marrow makes new red blood cells, germ-fighting white blood cells, and platelets that stop a cut from bleeding.

5 Part of the bone is made of bone tissue that looks like a dry sponge. It is made of strong, hard tubes. It is also found in the middle of short, flat bones.

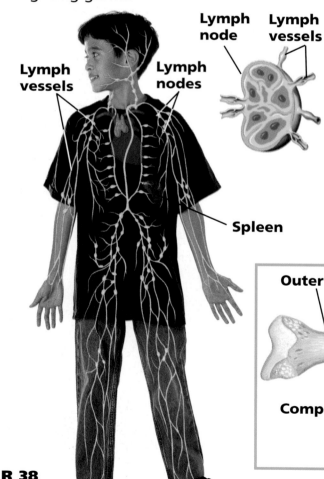

Lymph vessels

Lymph nodes

Lymph node

Lymph vessels

Spleen

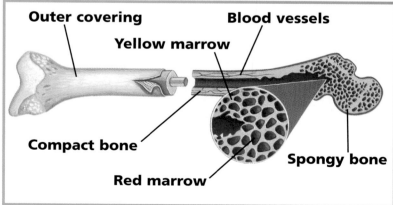

Outer covering

Blood vessels

Yellow marrow

Compact bone

Red marrow

Spongy bone

Infectious Diseases

A disease is anything that breaks down the normal functions of the body. Some diseases are inherited. Others are caused by harmful materials in the environment. Many diseases, however, are caused by organisms.

Disease-causing organisms include bacteria and viruses. Diseases caused by these organisms are called *infectious diseases* because the organisms enter, or infect, the body.

Human Infectious Diseases		
Disease	**Caused by**	**Organ System Affected**
Chicken pox	Virus	Skin
Smallpox	Virus	Skin
Polio	Virus	Nervous system
Rabies	Virus	Nervous system
Influenza	Virus	Respiratory system
Measles	Virus	Skin
Mumps	Virus	Salivary glands
Tuberculosis	Bacteria	Respiratory system
Tetanus	Bacteria	Nervous system
Food poisoning	Bacteria	Digestive system

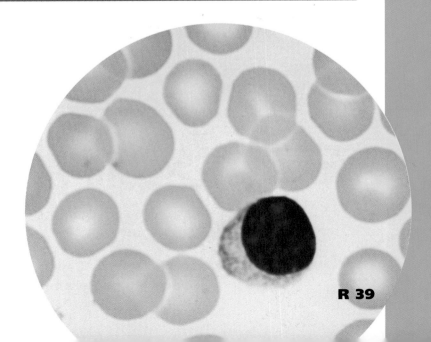

White blood cells are your body's main protection against infectious disease. The white blood cells leave the blood vessels or lymph vessels to fight disease organisms in your tissues.

Staying Healthy

Physical fitness is the condition in which the body is healthy and works the best it can. It involves working the skeletal muscles, bones, joints, heart, and respiratory system.

Occasionally
Inactive pastimes such as watching TV

2–3 times a week
Leisure activities such as gardening, golf, softball

3–5 times a week Aerobic activities such as swimming; sports activities such as basketball, handball

Daily Substitute activity for inactivity—take the stairs, walk instead of riding

Activity Pyramid

CARE!

- Stay active every day.
- Eat a balanced diet.
- Drink plenty of water—6 to 8 large glasses a day.

There is more to fitness than exercise. To make sure your body gets all the nutrients you need, you should eat a balanced diet. *A balanced diet* includes all the major food groups.

A balanced diet provides the calories, or energy from food, that you need to stay healthy. The number of calories needed varies from person to person, depending on their metabolism. *Metabolism* is the rate at which you burn energy. It is determined by weight, age, sex, and level of activity.

Fats, oils, and sweets
Use sparingly

Milk, yogurt, and cheese group
2–3 servings

Meat, poultry, fish, dry beans, eggs, and nuts group
2–3 servings

Vegetable group
3–5 servings

Fruit group
2–4 servings

Bread, cereal, rice, and pasta group
6–11 servings

Food Guide Pyramid

FOLDABLES™

by Dinah Zike

Folding Instructions

So how do you make a Foldables data organizer? The following pages offer step-by-step instructions—where and when to fold, where to cut—for making 11 basic Foldables data organizers. The instructions begin with the basic shapes, such as the hot dog fold, that were introduced on page xv.

Half-Book

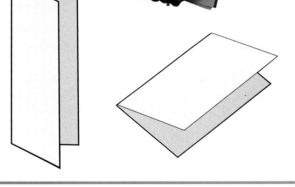

Fold a sheet of paper ($8\frac{1}{2}$" x 11") in half.

1. This book can be folded vertically like a hot dog or …

2. … it can be folded horizontally like a hamburger.

Folded Book

1. Make a Half-Book.

2. Fold in half again like a hamburger.

This makes a ready-made cover and two small pages inside for recording information.

Two-Tab Book

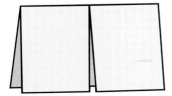

Take a Folded Book and cut up the valley of the inside fold toward the mountain top.

This cut forms two large tabs that can be used front and back for writing and illustrations.

Pocket Book

1. Fold a sheet of paper ($8\frac{1}{2}$" x 11") in half like a hamburger.

2. Open the folded paper and fold one of the long sides up two inches to form a pocket. Refold along the hamburger fold so that the newly formed pockets are on the inside.

3. Glue the outer edges of the two-inch fold with a small amount of glue.

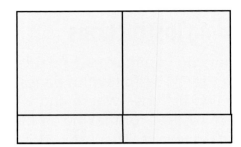

Shutter Fold

1. Begin as if you were going to make a hamburger, but instead of creasing the paper, pinch it to show the midpoint.

2. Fold the outer edges of the paper to meet at the pinch, or midpoint, forming a Shutter Fold.

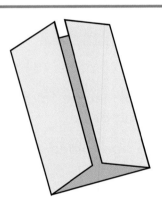

Trifold Book

1. Fold a sheet of paper ($8\frac{1}{2}$" x 11") into thirds.

2. Use this book as is, or cut into shapes.

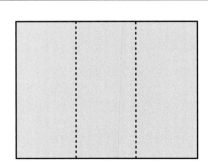

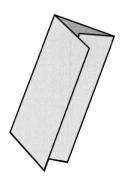

Three-Tab Book

1. Fold a sheet of paper like a hot dog.

2. With the paper horizontal and the fold of the hot dog up, fold the right side toward the center, trying to cover one half of the paper.

3. Fold the left side over the right side to make a book with three folds.

4. Open the folded book. Place one hand between the two thicknesses of paper and cut up the two valleys on one side only. This will create three tabs.

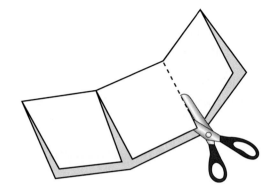

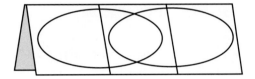

Layered-Look Book

1. Stack two sheets of paper ($8\frac{1}{2}$" x 11") so that the back sheet is one inch higher than the front sheet.

2. Bring the bottoms of both sheets upward and align the edges so that all of the layers or tabs are the same distance apart.

3. When all the tabs are an equal distance apart, fold the papers and crease well.

4. Open the papers and glue them together along the valley, or inner center fold, or staple them along the mountain.

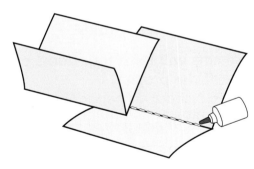

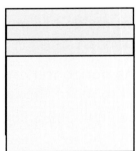

Four-Tab Book

1. Fold a sheet of paper ($8\frac{1}{2}$" x 11") in half like a hot dog.

2. Fold this long rectangle in half like a hamburger.

3. Fold both ends back to touch the mountain top or fold it like an accordion.

4. On the side with two valleys and one mountain top, make vertical cuts through one thickness of paper, forming four tabs.

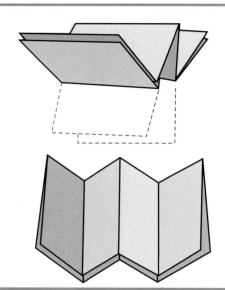

Four-Door Book

1. Make a Shutter Fold using 11" x 17" or 12" x 18" paper.

2. Fold the Shutter Fold in half like a hamburger. Crease well.

3. Open the project and cut along the two inside valley folds.

These cuts will form four doors on the inside of the project.

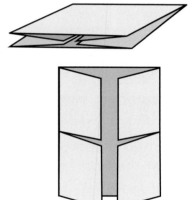

Folded Table or Chart

1. Fold the number of vertical columns needed to make the table or chart.

2. Fold the horizontal rows needed to make the table or chart.

3. Label the rows and columns.

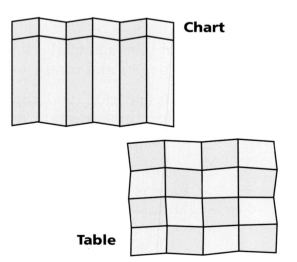

Chart

Table

Glossary

This Glossary will help you to pronounce and understand the meanings of the Science Words introduced in this book. The page number at the end of the definition tells where the word appears.

A

abiotic factor (ā′bī ot′ik fak′tər) A nonliving part of an ecosystem. (p. B6)

absorption (əb sôrp′shən) The disappearance of a sound wave into a surface. (p. F66)

abyssal plain (ə bis′əl plān) The vast flat lands beyond the continental shelf that cover almost half of the deep ocean floor. (p. C90)

acceleration (ak sel′ə rā′shən) Change in velocity with respect to time. (pp. F13, F22)

acid (as′id) A substance that tastes sour and turns blue litmus paper red. (p. E82)

acid rain (as′id rān) Moisture that falls to Earth after being mixed with wastes from burned fossil fuels. (p. C65)

acidity (ə sid′ə tē) The strength of an acid. (p. E86)

action (ak′shən) The force one object applies to a second, as in Newton's third law of motion, which states, "For every action, there is an equal but opposite reaction." *See* **reaction**. (p. F24)

adaptation (ad′əp tā′shən) A characteristic that enables a living thing to survive in its environment. (pp. A46, A106)

aerial root (âr′ē əl rüt) A root that never touches the ground but can take in moisture from the air. (p. A31)

aerosol (âr′ə sol′) A type of colloid in which liquid drops or solid particles are spread throughout a gas. (p. E60)

air mass (âr mas) A large region of the atmosphere where the air has similar properties throughout. (p. D70)

air pressure (âr presh′ər) The force put on a given area by the weight of the air above it. (p. D33)

alkalinity (al′kə lin′i tē) The strength of a base. (p. E86)

alternative energy source (ōl tûr′nə tiv en′ər jē sôrs) A source of energy other than the burning of a fossil fuel. (p. C104)

amphibian (am fib′ē ən) A vertebrate that lives part of its life in water and part of its life on land. (p. A95)

anemometer (an′ə mom′i tər) A device that measures wind speed. (p. D64)

PRONUNCIATION KEY

The following symbols are used throughout the McGraw-Hill Science Glossaries.

a	at	e	end	o	hot	u	up	hw	white	ə about
ā	ape	ē	me	ō	old	ū	use	ng	song	taken
ä	far	i	it	ôr	fork	ü	rule	th	thin	pencil
âr	care	ī	ice	oi	oil	u̇	pull	<u>th</u>	this	lemon
ô	law	îr	pierce	ou	out	ûr	turn	zh	measure	circus

′ = primary accent; shows which syllable takes the main stress, such as **kil** in **kilogram** (kil′ə gram′).

′ = secondary accent; shows which syllables take lighter stresses, such as **gram** in **kilogram.**

aneroid barometer (an'ə roid bə rom'i tər) A spring enclosed in a pleated metal can that expands or contracts to indicate changes in air pressure. (p. D34)

angiosperm (an'jē ə spûrm') A seed plant that produces flowers. *See* **gymnosperm**. (p. A68)

aquifer (ak'wə fər) An underground layer of rock or soil filled with water. (p. C75)

asexual reproduction (a sek'shü əl rē'prō duk'shən) The production of a new organism from only one cell. (p. A62)

asteroid (as'tə roid') "Minor planet." One of many small, rocky objects that orbit the Sun between the orbits of Mars and Jupiter. (p. D19)

asteroid belt (as'tə roid' belt) Region between Mars and Jupiter where most asteroids are found. (p. D19)

atmosphere (at'məs fîr') The blanket of gases that surrounds Earth. (pp. C26, D32)

atom (at'əm) The smallest unit of an element that retains the properties of that element. *See* **molecule**. (p. E26)

aurora (ə rôr'ə) The northern or southern lights that appear in the night sky, especially in polar regions. (p. D32)

B

bacterium (bak tîr'ē əm) *sing., n. pl.* **bacteria** (-ē ə) A member of either of two kingdoms of one-celled living things that have no nucleus, or center, in their cell body. (p. A19)

balanced forces (bal'ənst fôrs'əz) Forces that cancel each other out when acting together on a single object. (p. F21)

barometer (bə rom'i tər) A device for measuring air pressure. (p. D34)

base (bās) A substance that tastes bitter and turns red litmus paper blue. (p. E82)

basin (bās'in) The floor of an ocean, containing mountains, valleys, and plains. (p. C84)

bench mark (bench' märk') A plaque left by surveyors to tell the exact location and elevation of a place. (p. C6)

benthos (ben'thos) Organisms that live on the bottom in aquatic ecosystems. (p. B72)

bird (bûrd) A vertebrate that has both feathers and wings. (p. C95)

biomass (bī'ō mas') Energy from plant matter or animal waste. (p. C106)

biome (bī'ōm) One of Earth's large ecosystems, with its own kind of climate, soil, plants, and animals. (p. B64)

biotic factor (bī ot'ik fak'tər) A living part of an ecosystem. (p. B7)

boiling point (boil'ing point) The particular temperature for each substance at which it changes state from a liquid to a gas. (p. E37)

buoyancy (boi'ən sē) The upward push of a liquid on an object placed in it. (p. E12)

C

cambium (kam'bē əm) The layer in plants that separates the xylem from the phloem. (p. A31, A32)

camouflage (kam'ə fläzh') An adaptation in which an animal protects itself against predators by blending in with the environment. (p. A108)

carbon cycle (kär'bən si'kəl) The continuous exchange of carbon dioxide and oxygen among living things. (p. B53)

carnivore (kär'nə vôr') An animal that eats another animal. (p. B20)

carrying capacity (kar'ē ing kə pas'i tē) The maximum population size that an area can support. (p. B35)

cell (sel) The smallest unit of living matter. (p. A6)

chemical change (kem'i kəl chānj) A change of matter that occurs when atoms link together in a new way, creating a new substance different from the original substances. (p. E71)

chemical formula (kəm'i kəl fôr'myə lə) A way to write a compound's name using symbols. The letters tell what elements are in the compound, and the subscripts tell the number of particles in the compound. (p. E25)

chemical reaction (kem'i kəl rē ak'shən) Another name for chemical change. (p. E71)

chemosynthesis (kē'mō sin'thə sis) In tube worms the process by which bacteria create nutrients from hydrogen sulfide and oxygen, using chemical reactions rather than light. (p. C93)

chlorophyll (klôr'ə fil') A green chemical in plant cells that allows plants to use the Sun's energy for making food. (p. A6)

cirrus cloud (sir'əs kloud) A high-altitude cloud with a featherlike shape, made of ice crystals. (p. D44)

classification (klas'ə fi kā'shən) The science of finding patterns among living things. (p. A10)

cleavage (klē'vij) The tendency of a mineral to break along flat surfaces. (p. C34)

climate (klī'mit) The average weather pattern of a region. (p. D84)

climate zone (klī mat' zōn) A region that has similar weather patterns based on temperature, precipitation, wind, distance from a coast, mountain ranges, ocean currents, and vegetation. (p. D84)

climax community (klī'maks kə mū'ni tē) The final stage of succession in an area, unless a major change happens. (p. B84)

cold front (kōld frunt) A front where cold air moves in under a warm air mass. (p. D72)

colloid (kol'oid) A special type of mixture in which the particles of one material are scattered through another and block the passage of light without settling out. (pp. E54, E60)

comet (kom' it) A "dirty snowball" orbiting the Sun — a mixture of ices, frozen gases, rock, and dust left over from the formation of the solar system. (p. D19)

commensalism (kə men'sə liz'əm) A relationship between two kinds of organisms that benefits one without harming the other. (p. B27)

community (kə mū'ni tē) All the living things in an ecosystem. (p. B11)

complete flower (kəm plēt' flou'ər) A flower that has sepals, petals, stamens, and pistils. (p. A78)

compound (kom'pound) Any substance that is formed by the chemical combination of two or more elements and acts like a single substance. (p. E24)

compression (kəm presh'ən) **1.** The part of a sound wave where molecules are crowded together. (p. F51) **2.** A movement of plates that presses together or squeezes Earth's crust. (p. C8)

concave lens (kon kāv' lenz) A lens that is thicker at the edges than at the middle. As it curves inward, it spreads light rays apart, making images appear smaller. (p. F100)

concave mirror (kon kāv' mir'ər) A mirror that curves in on the shiny side. (p. F88)

condensation (kon'den sā'shən) *n.* The changing of a gas into a liquid. (pp. B50, D39) —**condense** (kən dens') *v.* (p. E37)

PRONUNCIATION KEY

a at; ā ape; ä far; âr care; ô law; e end; ē me; i it; ī ice; îr pierce; o hot; ō old; ôr fork; oi oil; ou out; u up; ū use; ü rule; ù pull; ûr turn; hw white; ng song; th thin; <u>th</u> this; zh measure; ə about, taken, pencil, lemon, circus

conduction (kən duk'shən) *n.* The passing of heat through a material while the material itself stays in place. (p. E97) —**conduct** (kən dukt') *v.* (p. E14)

conifer (kon'ə fər) Any of a group of gymnosperms that produce seeds in cones and have needlelike leaves. (p. A69)

conserve (kən'sûrv') To save, protect, or use resources wisely. (p. C39)

constellation (kon'stə lā'shən) Patterns formed by groups of stars in the night sky. (p. D12)

consumer (kən sü'mər) Any animal that eats plants or eats other plant-eating animals. (pp. B7, B20)

continental rise (kon'tə nen'təl rīz) A buildup of sediment on the sea floor at the bottom of the continental slope. It is a zone of sand and mud that stretches from the slope down to the deep-sea floor. (p. C90)

continental shelf (kon'tə nen'təl shelf) The underwater edge of a continent. (p. C90)

continental slope (kon'tə nen'təl slōp) The steep slope leading down from the continental shelf toward the sea floor. (p. C90)

contour plowing (kon'tür plou'ing) Preventing erosion by plowing across rather than up and down a slope. (p. C51)

contract (kən trakt') To shrink, as when a material gets colder. (p. E41)

convection (kən vek'shən) The flow of heat through a liquid or a gas, causing hot parts to rise and cooler parts to sink. (p. E97)

convection cell (kən vek'shən sel) A circular pattern of air rising, air sinking, and wind. (p. D55)

convex lens (kon veks' lenz) A lens that is thicker at the middle than at the edges. As it curves outward, it brings light together, making images appear larger. (p. F100)

convex mirror (kon veks' mir'ər) A mirror that curves out on the shiny side. (p. F88)

coquina (kō kē'nə) A sedimentary rock formed from seashell fragments. (p. C44)

Coriolis effect (kôr'ē ō'lis i fekt') The curving of the path of a moving object caused by Earth's rotation. (p. D57)

cortex (kôr'teks) The layer of tissue just inside the epidermis of a plant's roots and stems. (p. A30)

cotyledon (ko'tə lē'dən) A tiny leaflike structure, also called a seedleaf, inside the seed of an angiosperm. (p. A72)

crop rotation (krop rō tā'shən) Growing different crops each year so that the soil does not use up the same kinds of minerals year after year. (p. C51)

crossbreeding (krôs'brēd'ing) Producing offspring by mating individuals from two distinct breeds or varieties of the same species. (p. A112)

cross-pollination (krôs'pol'ə nā'shən) The transfer of pollen from one flower to another. (p. A80)

crust (krust) The rocky surface that makes up the top of the lithosphere and includes the continents and the ocean floor. (p. C7)

crystal (kris'təl) The geometric shape a mineral forms when its atoms and molecules get into fixed patterns. (p. C32)

cumulus cloud (kū'myə ləs kloud) A puffy cloud that appears to rise up from a flat bottom. (p. D44)

current (kûr'ənt) An ocean movement; a large stream of water that flows in the ocean. (p. C86)

cycad (sī'kad) One of the evergreen gymnosperms that resemble palms and have seed-bearing cones. (p. A69)

decibel (dB) (des'ə bel') A unit that measures loudness. (p. F58)

deciduous (di sij´ü əs) Said of a plant that loses its leaves each fall. *See* **evergreen**. (pp. A69, B70)

deciduous forest (di si´jə wəs fôr´ist) A forest biome with many kinds of trees that lose their leaves each autumn. (p. B70)

decomposer (dē´kəm pōz´ər) Any of the fungi or bacteria that break down dead plants and animals into useful things like minerals and rich soil. (pp. B7, B21, B56)

delta (del´tə) Fan-shaped region formed by deposits of sediments found at the mouth of a river. (p. C21)

density (den´si tē) A measure of how tightly packed the matter in an object is. (pp. C35, E8)

deposition (dep´ə zish´ən) The dropping off of bits of eroded rock. (p. C13)

desalination (dē sal´ə nā´shən) Getting fresh water from seawater. (p. C73)

desert (dez´ərt) A sandy or rocky biome, with little precipitation and little plant life. (p. B69)

dicot (dī´kot´) An angiosperm with two cotyledons in each seed. *See* **monocot**. (p. A72)

dinoflagellate (din´ə flaj´ə lāt´) A protist containing chlorophyll that has two flagella for motion. When they overreproduce, they can cause "red tides." (p. A14)

distillation (dis´tə lā´shən) The process of separating the parts of a mixture by evaporation and condensation. (p. E64)

diversity (di vûr´si tē) A wide variety of traits in individuals from the same population. (p. A114)

Doppler effect (dop´lər i fekt´) The change in frequency (and pitch) as a source of sound moves toward or away from you. (p. F71)

downdraft (doun´draft´) A downward rush of air caused by the falling of rain during a thunderstorm. (pp. D55, D76)

echo (e´kō) A reflected sound wave. (p. F68)

echolocation (ek´ō lō kā´shən) Finding an object by using reflected sound. (p. F70)

ecological succession (ek´ə loj´i kəl sək sesh´ən) The gradual replacement of one community by another. (p. B82)

ecology (ē kol´ə jē) The study of how living and nonliving things interact. (p. B11)

ecosystem (ek´ō sis´təm) All the living and nonliving things in an environment, including their interactions with each other. (p. B6)

effort arm (ef´ərt arm) The part of a lever that applies force to the resistance arm. (p. F26)

electromagnetic spectrum (i lek´trō mag net´ik spek´trəm) All the wavelengths of visible and invisible light in order, from short (gamma rays) to long (radio). (p. F119)

electromagnetism (i lek´trō mag´ni tiz´əm) The production of magnetism by electricity (and the production of electricity by magnets). (p. F118)

electron (i lek´tron) A particle in the space outside the nucleus of an atom that carries one unit of negative electric charge. (p. E27)

element (el´ə mənt) A pure substance that cannot be broken down into any simpler substances. (p. E22)

PRONUNCIATION KEY

a at; ā ape; ä far; âr care; ô law; e end; ē me; i it; ī ice; îr pierce; o hot; ō old; ôr fork; oi oil; ou out; u up; ū use; ü rule; ù pull; ûr turn; hw white; ng song; th thin; th this; zh measure; ə about, taken, pencil, lemon, circus

elevation (el′ə vā′shən) The height of a place above sea level. (p. C6)

embryo (em′brē ō′) The immature plant inside a seed. (p. A82)

emulsion (i mul′shən) A type of colloid in which one liquid is spread throughout another. (p. E60)

endangered species (en dān′jərd spē′shēz) A species that is in danger of becoming extinct. (p. B36)

epidermis (ep′i dûr′mis) An outermost layer of such plant parts as roots and leaves. (pp. A30, A34)

erosion (i rō′zhən) The picking up and carrying away of pieces of rocks. (p. C10)

evaporation (i vap′ə rā′shən) The slow changing of a liquid into a gas. (pp. B50, D38, E38)

evergreen (ev′ər grēn′) Said of a gymnosperm that keeps its leaves for at least a few years. *See* **deciduous**. (p. A69)

expand (ek spand′) To spread out, as when a material gets hotter. (p. E41)

extinct (ek stingkt′) A species that has died out completely. (p. B36)

F

fault (fôlt) A crack in Earth's crust whose sides show evidence of motion. (p. C6)

fault-block mountain (fôlt blok moun′tən) A mountain formed by blocks of Earth's crust moving along a fault. (p. C9)

fertilization (fûr′tə lə zā′shən) The joining of a sperm cell with an egg cell to make one new cell, a fertilized egg. (pp. A62, A81)

fertilizer (fûr′tə lī′zər) A substance used to add minerals to the soil. (p. B56)

fibrous root (fī′brəs rüt) One of the many hairy branching roots that some plants have. (p. A31)

filament (fil′ə mənt) The wire in a light bulb that gives off light and heat. (p. E92)

fish (fish) A vertebrate that lives its whole life in water. (p. A95)

flood plain (flud′ plān′) Land that is likely to be underwater during a flood. (p. C21)

foam (fōm) A type of colloid in which a gas is spread throughout a liquid. (p. E60)

fog (fôg) A cloud at ground level. (p. D44)

fold mountain (fōld moun′tən) A mountain made up mostly of rock layers folded by being squeezed together. (p. C8)

food chain (füd chān) The path of the energy in food from one organism to another. (p. B18)

food web (füd web) The overlapping food chains in an ecosystem. (p. B20)

force (fôrs) A push or pull exerted by one object on another, causing a change in motion. (p. F6)

fossil (fos′əl) Any remains or imprint of living things of the past. (p. C45)

fossil fuel (fos′əl fū′əl) A fuel formed from the decay of ancient forms of life. (p. C64)

fracture (frak′chər) The characteristic way some minerals break in uneven patterns. (p. C35)

freezing point (frēz′ing point) The temperature at which a substance changes state from a liquid to a solid. (p. E37)

frequency (frē′kwən sē) The number of times an object vibrates per second. (p. F57)

friction (frik′ shen′) A force that opposes the motion of one object moving past another. (p. F8)

frond (frond) The leaf of a fern. (p. A61)

front (frunt) A boundary between air masses with different temperatures. (p. D71)

fruit (früt) The ripened ovary of a flowering seed plant. (p. A70)

fulcrum (fúl′krəm) The pivot point of a lever. (p. F26)

fundamental frequency (fun′də men′təl frē′kwən sē) The lowest frequency at which an object vibrates. (p. F72)

fungus (fung′gəs) *n.,* **fungi** (fun′jī) *pl.* Members of a kingdom that contains one-celled and many-celled living things that absorb food from their environment. (p. A17)

G

galaxy (gal′ək sē) A collection of billions of stars. Our Sun belongs to the Milky Way galaxy. (p. D20)

gas (gas) A form of matter that does not take up a definite amount of space and has no definite shape. (p. E36)

gel (jel) A type of colloid in which a solid is spread throughout a liquid. (p. E60)

gem (jem) A mineral valued for being rare and beautiful. (p. C38)

geologist (jē ol′ə jist) A scientist who studies rocks to tell how they formed and to predict when an earthquake may occur. (p. C16)

geothermal energy (jē′ō thûr′məl en′ər jē) Earth's internal energy. (p. C104)

germination (jûr′mə nā′shən) The sprouting of a seed into a new plant. (p. A83)

ginkgo (ging′kō) *n., pl.* **ginkgoes** A large gymnosperm with fan-shaped leaves. (p. A69)

gnetophyte (ne′tō fīt′) One of the gymnosperms that are closely related to flowering plants and live in both deserts and the tropics. (p. A69)

grassland (gras′land′) A biome where grasses, not trees, are the main plant life. Prairies are one kind of grassland region. (p. B66)

gravitropism (grav′ī trō′pi′zəm) The response of a plant to gravity. (p. A44)

gravity (grav′i tē) The force of attraction between any two objects due to their mass. (pp. D8, F35)

groundwater (ground wô′tər) Precipitation that seeps into the ground and is stored in tiny holes, or pores, in soil and rocks. (pp. B51, C74)

gymnosperm (jim′nə spûrm′) A seed plant that does not produce flowers. *See* **angiosperm**. (p. A68)

H

habitat (hab′i tat) The place where a plant or animal naturally lives and grows. (p. B12)

hail (hāl) Pellets made of ice and snow. (p. D47)

hardness (härd′nis) How well a mineral resists scratching. (p. C34)

herbivore (hûr′bə vôr′) An animal that eats plants, algae, and other producers. (p. B20)

heredity (hə red′i tē) The passing down of inherited traits from parents to offspring. (p. A110)

hertz (Hz) (hûrts) A unit for measuring frequency. One hertz equals a frequency of one vibration per second. (p. F57)

heterogeneous (het′ər ə jē′nē əs) Differing in kind or nature; dissimilar; not homogeneous. (p. E54)

high-pressure system (hī′presh′ər sis′təm) A pattern surrounding a high pressure center, from which winds blow outward. In the Northern Hemisphere these winds curve to the right in a clockwise pattern. (p. D59)

PRONUNCIATION KEY

a at; ā ape; ä far; âr care; ô law; e end; ē me; i it; ī ice; îr pierce; o hot; ō old; ôr fork; oi oil; ou out; u up; ū use; ü rule; u̇ pull; ûr turn; hw white; ng song; th thin; <u>th</u> this; zh measure; ə about, taken, pencil, lemon, circus

host (hōst) The organism a parasite lives in or on and is harmed by. (p. B26)

humidity (hū mid′i tē) The amount of water vapor in the air. (p. D38)

humus (hü′məs) Decayed plant or animal material in soil. (pp. B9, C49)

hurricane (hûr′i kān′) A very large, swirling storm with very low pressure at the center. (p. D78)

hybrid (hī′brid) An organism produced by the crossing of parents that have different forms of the same trait. (p. A112)

hydrocarbon (hī′drə kär′bən) Compound made only of hydrogen and carbon atoms. (p. E32)

hydroelectric plant (hī′drō i lek′trik plant) A factory where running or falling water spins a generator to make electricity. (p. C104)

hydrosphere (hī′drə sfîr′) Earth's water, found in continents and oceans, including the fresh water in ice, lakes, rivers, and underground water. (p. C26)

hydrotropism (hī drot′rə piz′əm) The response of a plant to a nearby source of water. (p. A45)

hyperthermia (hī′pər thûr′mē ə) The overheating of the body that can be caused by overexposure in a hot, dry climate. (p. D90)

I

igneous rock (ig′nē əs rok) A rock formed when melted rock material cools and hardens (p. C43)

image (im′ij) A "picture" of the light source that light rays make in bouncing off a polished, shiny surface. (p. F89)

imperfect flower (im pûr′fikt flou′ər) A flower with either a stamen or a pistil, but not both. (p. A78)

incomplete flower (in′kəm plēt′ flou′ər) A flower that lacks sepals, petals, stamens or pistils. (p. A78)

indicator (in′di kā′tər) A substance such as litmus paper whose color changes when it is mixed with an acid or a base. (p. E84)

inertia (i nûr′shə) The tendency of a moving object to keep moving in a straight line or of any object to resist a change in motion. (pp. D8, F7)

inexhaustible resource (in′eg zôs′tə bəl rē′sôrs′) A resource that cannot be depleted or used up easily. (p. B58)

inherited trait (in her′i təd trāt) A characteristic that is passed from parents to offspring. (p. A110)

inner planet (in′ər plan′it) A planet between the Sun and the asteroid belt (Mercury, Venus, Earth, Mars). (p. D16)

insolation (in′sə lā′shən) The amount of the Sun's energy that reaches Earth at a given time and place. *Insolation* is short for *in*coming *sol*ar radi*ation*. (p. D30)

instinct (in′stingkt′) An inherited behavior, one that is not learned but is done automatically. (p. A110)

insulate (in′sə lāt′) To prevent heat from passing through. (p. E14)

intertidal zone (in′tər tī′dəl zōn) The shallowest section of the marine, or ocean, ecosystem, where the ocean floor is covered and uncovered as the tide goes in and out. (p. B73)

invertebrate (in vûr′tə brit) An animal that does not have a backbone. (p. A16)

ionized (ī′ə nīzd′) Electrically charged by radiation, as gas particles of auroras in the night sky. (p. D32)

isobar (ī′sə bär′) A line on a weather map connecting places with equal air pressure. (p. D59)

kinetic energy (ki net′ik en′ər jē) The energy of any moving object. (p. E95)

land breeze (land brēz) Wind that blows from land to sea. (p. D56)

laser (lā'zər) A device that produces a thin stream of light of just a few close wavelengths. (p. F122)

lava (lä'və) Magma that reaches Earth's surface. (pp. C9, C43)

law of reflection (lô uv ri flek'shən) The angle between an incoming light ray and a surface equals the angle between the reflected light ray and the surface. (p. F87)

lever (lev'ər) A simple machine made of a rigid bar and a fixed pivot point, called the fulcrum. (p. F26)

light ray (līt rā) A straight-line beam of light as it travels outward from its source. (p. F85)

lightning (līt'ning) One of the huge electric sparks that leap from clouds to the ground in thunderstorms. (p. D76)

limiting factor (lim'ə ting fak'tər) Anything that controls the growth or survival of a population. (p. B34)

liquid (lik'wid) A form of matter that takes up a definite amount of space and has no definite shape. (p. E36)

lithosphere (lith'ə sfîr') The hard outer layer of Earth, about 100 km thick. (p. C26)

long-day plant (lông'dā plant) A plant that blooms when there is much more daylight than darkness. (p. A46)

low-pressure system (lō'presh'ər sis'təm) A pattern surrounding a low-pressure center, in which winds blow in toward the center. In the Northern Hemisphere, these winds blow to the right in a counterclockwise pattern. (p. D59)

luster (lus'tər) The way light bounces off a mineral's surface. (p. C33)

magma (mag'mə) Hot, molten rock deep below Earth's surface. (p. C9)

magnetic (mag net'ik) The property of a material like iron in which the particles line up pole to pole, causing it to be attracted or repelled by a magnet. (p. E15)

mammal (mam'əl) A vertebrate that feeds its young milk. (p. A95)

mare (mär'ā) *n., pl.* **maria** (mär'ē ə) Dark-colored land on the Moon that is dry and flat and is surrounded by mountains and ridges. (p. D10)

mass (mas) A measure of the amount of matter in an object. (p. E6)

matter (ma'tər) Anything that has mass and takes up space. (pp. E6, F51)

meander (mē an'dər) Bends or s-shaped curves in a river. (p. C21)

melting point (melt'ing point) The particular temperature for each substance at which it changes state from a solid to a liquid. (p. E37)

membrane (mem'brān) A thin envelope surrounding the nucleus of a cell. (p. A18)

metal (met'əl) Any of a group of elements found in the ground that conducts heat and electricity. (p. C38)

PRONUNCIATION KEY

a at; ā ape; ä far; âr care; ô law; e end; ē me; i it; ī ice; îr pierce; o hot; ō old; ôr fork; oi oil; ou out; u up; ū use; ü rule; ù pull; ûr turn; hw white; ng song; th thin; <u>th</u> this; zh measure; ə about, taken, pencil, lemon, circus

metamorphic rock (met′ə môr′fik rok) A rock formed under heat and pressure from another kind of rock. (p. C46)

meteor (mē′ tē or) A chunk of rock from space that burns up as it travels through Earth's atmosphere. A "shooting star." (p. D19)

meteorite (mē′tē ə rīt′) A chunk of rock from space that strikes the surface of Earth or the Moon. (pp. C14, D19)

mid-ocean ridge (mid ō′shun rij) Chain of mountains that wind along all the world's major oceans. (p. C91)

mimicry (mim′i krē) An adaptation in which an animal is protected against predators by its resemblance to another, unpleasant animal. (p. A106)

mineral (min′ə rəl) A solid material of Earth's crust with a definite composition. (p. C32)

mixture (miks′chər) A physical combination of two or more substances that are blended together without forming new substances. (p. E52)

molecule (mol′ə kūl′) A particle that contains more than one atom joined together. (p. E30) *See* **atom**. (p. E26)

monocot (mon′ə kot′) An angiosperm with one cotyledon in each seed. *See* **dicot**. (p. A72)

mountain breeze (moun′tən brēz) A cool night wind that blows down a mountain slope to replace the warmer air in the valley. (p. D56)

mutualism (mū′chü ə liz′əm) A relationship between two kinds of organisms that benefits both. (p. B24)

N

neap tide (nēp tīd) The slightest changes from high to low tide that occur when the Sun, the Moon, and Earth form a right angle or are perpendicular to each other. (p. C89)

nekton (nek′tən) Organisms that swim through the water in aquatic ecosystems. (p. B72)

neutral (nü′trəl) Neither acid nor base. (p. E82)

neutron (nü′tron) A particle in the nucleus of an atom that has no net electric charge. (p. E27)

newton (nü′tən) A basic unit measuring the amount of pull or push a force produces. (pp. E7, F20)

NEXRAD (neks′rad′) A new form of Doppler radar that is used to track storms. The word stands for *NEXt generation of weather RADar.* (p. D81)

niche (nich) The role of an organism in a community. (p. B12)

nitrogen cycle (nī′trə jən sī′kəl) The continuous trapping of nitrogen gas into compounds in the soil and its return to the air. (p. B54)

nonrenewable resource (non′ri nü′ə bəl rē′sôrs′) A resource that cannot be replaced within a short period of time or at all. (pp. B58, C64)

nonvascular (non vas′kyə lər) Containing no plant tissue through which water and food move. (p. A15)

nucleus (nü′klē əs) 1. A dense structure inside the cell. (p. A18) 2. One of the airborne dust particles around which water condenses as droplets or ice crystals before falling as precipitation. (p. D46) 3. An atom's dense center, where most of its mass is. (p. E27)

O

omnivore (om′nə vôr′) An animal that eats both plants and animals. (p. B21)

opaque (ō pāk′) Completely blocking light from passing through it. (p. F96)

orbit (ôr′bit) The path of a planet traveling around a star. (p. D6)

ore (ôr) A mineral containing a useful substance. (p. C38)

organ (ôr′gən) A group of tissues that work together to do a certain job. (p. A9)

organism (ôr′gə niz′əm) Any living thing that can carry out its life on its own. (p. A6)

organ system (ôr′gən sis′təm) A group of organs that work together to do a certain job. (p. A9)

outer planet (out′er plan′it) One of the five planets beyond the asteroid belt (Jupiter, Saturn, Uranus, Neptune, Pluto). (p. D16)

ovary (ō′və rē) A structure containing egg cells; the base of a pistil in a flower. (p. A78)

overtone (ō′vər tōn′) One of a series of pitches that blend to give a sound its quality. (p. F72)

ozone layer (ō′zōn lā′ər) A layer of ozone gas in the atmosphere that screens out much of the Sun's UV (ultraviolet) rays. (p. C63)

parasitism (par′ə sī tiz′əm) A relationship in which one organism lives in or on another organism and benefits from that relationship while the other organism may be harmed by it. (p. B26) —**parasite** (par′ə sīt′) (pp. A71, B26)

perfect flower (pûr′fikt flou′ər) A flower with both male and female parts, that is, both a stamen and a pistil. (p. A78)

permafrost (pûr′mə frôst′) A layer of permanently frozen soil found in arctic and antarctic regions. (p. B68)

pH (pē′aitch′) The scale that tells how acidic or basic a solution is. (p. E86)

phloem (flō′em) The tissue through which food from the leaves moves down through the rest of a plant. (pp. A31, A32)

photon (fō′ton) The tiny bundles of energy by means of which light travels. (p. F119)

photoperiodism (fō′tō pîr′ē ə diz′əm) The flowering response of a plant to changing periods of daylight and darkness. (p. A46)

photosynthesis (fō′tə sin′thə sis) The food-making process in green plants that uses sunlight. (p. A36)

phototropism (fō tot′rə piz′əm) The response of a plant to changes in light. (p. A44)

phylum (fī′ləm) *n., pl.* **phyla** (-lə) One of the large groups in the animal kingdom. (p. A16)

physical change (fiz′i kəl chānj) A change of matter in size, shape, or state without any change in identity. (p. E70)

pioneer community (pī′ə nîr′ kə mū′ni tē) The first community thriving in a once lifeless area. (p. B83)

pioneer species (pī′ə nîr′ spē′shēz) The first species living in an otherwise lifeless area. (p. B83)

pitch (pich) How high or low a sound is. (p. F56)

planet (plan′it) Any of the nine major objects that travel around the Sun and shine by reflecting its light. (p. D6)

plankton (plangk′tən) Organisms that float on the water in aquatic ecosystems. (p. B72)

plate (plāt) One of the moving pieces of Earth's crust that has been broken by upward pressure from the mantle. (p. C7)

plate tectonics (plāt tek ton′iks) A scientific theory that Earth's crust is made of moving plates. (pp. B90, C7)

polarization (pō′lər ə zā′shən) Allowing light vibrations to pass through in only one direction. (p. F97)

pollen (pol′ən) Dustlike grains in the flower of a plant that contain its male sex cells. (pp. A70, A74, A84)

PRONUNCIATION KEY

a **at**; ā **ape**; ä **far**; âr **care**; ô **law**; e **end**; ē **me**; i **it**; ī **ice**; îr **pierce**; o **hot**; ō **old**; ôr **fork**; oi **oil**; ou **out**; u **up**; ū **use**; ü **rule**; ú **pull**; ûr **turn**; hw **white**; ng **song**; th **thin**; <u>th</u> **this**; zh **measure**; ə **about, taken, pencil, lemon, circus**

pollination (pol′ə nā′shən) The transfer of a pollen grain to the egg-producing part of a plant. (p. A74)

pollute (pə lüt′) *v.* To add harmful substances to Earth's land, water, or air. (p. C50) **—pollutant** (pə lü′tənt) *n.* Something that pollutes. (p. C50) **—pollution** (pə lü′shən) *n.* A polluted condition. (p. C50)

population (pop′yə lā′shən) All the members of one species in an area. (p. B11)

potential energy (pə ten′shəl en′ər jē) Stored energy. (p. E95)

precipitation (pri sip′i tā′shən) Any form of water particles that falls from the atmosphere and reaches the ground. (pp. B51, D46)

predator (pred′ə tər) An animal that hunts other animals for food. (pp. A106, B21)

prey (prā) A living thing that is hunted for food. (p. B21)

primary color (prī′mer′ē kul′ər) Red, green, or blue. Mixing these colors can produce all the colors of the spectrum. (p. F110)

primary pigment (prī′mer′ē pig′mənt) Magenta, cyan, or yellow. Materials with any of these colors absorb one primary color of light and reflect the other two. (p. F112)

primary succession (prī′mer′ē sək sesh′ən) The beginning of a community where few, if any, living things exist, or where earlier communities were wiped out. (p. B82)

prism (priz′əm) A cut piece of clear glass (or plastic) with two opposite sides in the shape of a triangle or other geometric shape. (p. F108)

producer (prə dü′sər) Any of the plants and algae that produce oxygen and food that animals need. (pp. B7, B20)

product (prod′ukt) A new substance produced by a chemical change. (p. E71)

prop root (prop rüt) One of the roots that grow out of a plant's stemlike main roots and help prop up the plant. (p. A31)

property (prop′ər tē) A characteristic of matter that can be observed, such as mass, volume, weight, or density. (pp. E6, E24)

protective coloration (prə tek′tiv kul′ə rā′shən) A type of camouflage in which the color of an animal blends in with its background, protecting it against predators. (p. A109)

protein (prō′tēn) A substance rich in nitrogen that the body uses for growth and the repair of cells. (p. B54)

protist (prō′tist) A member of a kingdom that contains one-celled and many-celled living things, some that make food and some that hunt for food. (p. A18)

proton (prō′ton) A particle in the nucleus of an atom that carries one unit of positive electric charge. (p. E27)

Q

quality (kwol′i tē) The difference you hear between two sounds of the same loudness and pitch. (p. F72)

R

radar (rā′där) A device for tracking the position and path of a distant moving object. (p. D80)

radiation (rā′dē a′shən) The transfer of heat through electromagnetic rays. (p. E97)

rarefaction (râr′ə fak′shən) The part of a sound wave where molecules are spread apart. (p. F51)

raw material (râ mə tîr′ē əl) Material not yet refined, manufactured, or processed. (p. B58)

reactant (rē ak′tənt) An original substance at the beginning of a chemical reaction. (p. E71)

reaction (rē ak′shən) The force with which an object responds to an action, as in Newton's third law of motion. (p. F24)

reflection (ri flek′shən) The bouncing of a sound wave off a surface. (p. F66)

refraction (ri frak′shən) The bending of light rays as they pass from one substance into another. (p. F98)

relative humidity (rel′ə tiv hū mid′i tē) A comparison between how much water vapor is in the air and how much the air could hold at a given temperature if it were full, or saturated. (p. D39)

renewable resource (ri nü′ə bəl rē′sôrs′) A resource that can be replaced in a short period of time. (pp. B58, C62)

reservoir (rez′ər vwär′) A storage area for fresh water supplies. (p. C75)

resistance arm (ri zis′təns arm) The part of a lever that applies force to the load the machine acts against. (p. F26)

resonance (rez′ə nəns) In an instrument or object, a unique blend of the fundamental frequency and its overtones. (p. F72)

resource (rē′sôrs′) Any material that helps support life on Earth. (p. C26)

respiration (res′pə rā′shən) The release of energy in plants and animals from food (sugar). (p. A37)

response (ri spons′) What a living thing does as a result of a stimulus. (p. A44)

reptile (rep′təl) An egg-laying vertebrate with thick, dry skin. (p. A95)

revolve (ri volv′) To move around, or orbit, another object. (p. D10)

rhizoid (rī′zoid) One of the hairlike fibers that anchor a moss to the soil and take in water from the soil. (p. A58)

rhizome (rī′zōm) The underground stem of a fern. (p. A61)

rock (rok) A naturally formed solid in the crust made up of one or more minerals. (p. C42)

rock cycle (rok sī′kəl) Rocks changing from one into another in a never-ending series of processes. (p. C52)

root cap (rüt kap) A thin covering made up of cells that protect the root tip of a plant as it grows into the soil. (p. A30)

root hair (rüt hâr) Any of the threadlike projections from a plant root that absorb water and dissolved minerals from the soil. (p. A30)

rotate (rō′tāt) To make a complete spin on an axis, causing one day on a planet. A day differs in length from planet to planet. (p. D9)

runoff (run′ôf) Precipitation that flows across the land's surface or falls into rivers and streams. (pp. B51, C20)

S

savanna (sə van′ə) A tropical grassland with some trees and shrubs. (p. B66)

scanning tunneling microscope (scan′ing tun′əl ing mī′krə skōp′) A device that uses electric current flowing through a needle to trace the contours of atoms and magnify them as much as 30 million times. (p. E26)

scavenger (skav′ən jər) A meat-eating animal that feeds on the remains of dead animals. (p. B21)

sea breeze (sē brēz) Wind that blows from sea to land. (p. D56)

sea-floor vent (sē′flôr′ vent) An opening in a mid-ocean ridge where mineral-saturated water boils up from the seafloor crust. (p. C93)

seamount (sē′mount′) A huge underwater volcanic mountain that may emerge from the ocean surface as an island. (p. C90)

PRONUNCIATION KEY

a **at**; ā **ape**; ä **far**; âr **care**; ô **law**; e **end**; ē **me**; i **it**; ī **ice**; îr **pierce**; o **hot**; ō **old**; ôr **fork**; oi **oil**; ou **out**; u **up**; ū **use**; ü **rule**; ù **pull**; ûr **turn**; hw **white**; ng **song**; th **thin**; th **this**; zh **measure**; ə **about, taken, pencil, lemon, circus**

secondary succession (sek'ən der'ē sək sesh'ən) The beginning of a new community where an earlier community already exists. (p. B82)

sediment (sed'ə ment) Pieces of material carried and deposited by water or wind (p. C20)

sedimentary rock (sed'ə men'tə rē rok) A rock made of bits of matter joined together. (p. C44)

seed (sēd) An undeveloped plant with stored food sealed in a protective covering. (p. A68)

seed coat (sēd kōt) The outer covering of a seed. (p. A82)

seed dispersal (sēd di spûr'səl) The movement of a seed from the flower to a place where it can sprout. (p. A83)

self-pollination (self'pol'ə nā'shən) The transfer of pollen from an anther to a stigma in the same plant. (p. A80)

sexual reproduction (sek'shü əl rē'prō duk'shən) The production of a new organism from a female sex cell and a male sex cell. (pp. A62, A81)

shear (shîr) A movement of plates that twists, tears, or pushes one part of Earth's crust past another. (p. C8)

short-day plant (shôrt'dā plant) A plant that blooms when there is more darkness and less daylight. (p. A46)

simple machine (sim'pəl mə shēn') A machine with few moving parts, making it easier to do work. (p. F26)

smog (smog) A mixture of smoke and fog. (p. C64)

solar system (sō'lər sis'təm) The Sun and the objects that are traveling around it. (p. D6)

solid (sol'id) A form of matter that has a definite shape and takes up a definite amount of space. (p. E36)

solubility (sol'yə bil'i tē) The ability of a substance to be dissolved by another substance. (p. E58)

solute (sol'ūt) A substance that is dissolved by another substance to form a solution. (p. E57)

solution (sə lü'shən) A mixture of substances that are blended so completely that the mixture looks the same everywhere. (p. E54)

solvent (sol'vənt) A substance that dissolves one or more other substances to form a solution. (p. E57)

sound wave (sound wāv) A vibration that spreads away from a vibrating object. (p. F51)

spectrum (spek'trəm) A band of colors produced when light goes through a prism. (p. F108)

speed (spēd) How fast an object's position changes with time at any given moment. (p. F11)

spore (spôr) Cells in seedless plants that grow into new organisms. (p. A58)

spring (spring) A place where groundwater seeps out of the ground. (p. C75)

spring tide (spring tīd) The greatest changes from high to low tide that occur when the Sun, the Moon, and Earth are lined up. (p. C89)

state of matter (stāt uv mat'ər) One of the three forms that matter can take—solid, liquid, or gas. (p. E36)

stimulus (stim'yə ləs), *n., pl.* **stimuli (-lī)** Something in the environment that causes a living thing to react. (p. A44)

stomata (stō'mə tə) *pl. n., sing.* **stoma** Pores in the bottom of leaves that open and close to let in air or give off water vapor. (p. A34)

storm surge (stôrm sûrj) A great rise of the sea along a shore caused by low air pressure. (p. D79)

stratus cloud (strā'təs kloud) A cloud that forms in a blanketlike layer. (p. D44)

streak (strēk) The color of the powder left when a mineral is rubbed against a hard, rough surface. (p. C34)

strip farming (strip fär′ming) Trapping runoff by alternating tightly growing grasses with more widely spaced plants. (p. C51)

subscript (sub′skript′) A number in a chemical formula that tells the number of atoms in the compound. (p. E25)

surveyor (sər vā′ər) A specialist who makes accurate measurements of Earth's crust. (p. C6)

suspension (sə spen′shən) A mixture in which suspended particles can easily be seen. (p. E59)

symbiosis (sim′bē ō′sis) A relationship between two kinds of organisms that lasts over time. (p. B24)

taiga (tī′gə) A cool forest biome of conifers in the upper Northern Hemisphere. (p. B67)

taproot (tap′rüt′) A root that has few hairy branches and grows deep into the ground. (p. A31)

temperate (tem′pər it) Free from extremes of temperature. (p. B66)

tension (ten′shən) A movement of plates that stretches or pulls apart Earth's crust. (p. C8)

terracing (ter′is ing) Shaping hillsides into steps so that runoff and eroded soil get trapped on the steps. (p. C51)

texture (teks′chər) An identifying quality of a rock based on how coarse, fine, or glassy it is and on how angular or rounded it is. (p. C42)

threatened species (thret′ənd spē′shēz) A species that is in danger of becoming endangered. (p. D36)

thunder (thun′dər) The noise caused by lightning-heated air during a thunderstorm. (p. D76)

thunderhead (thun′dər hed′) A cumulonimbus cloud in which a thunderstorm forms. (p. D76)

thunderstorm (thun′dər stôrm′) The most common severe storm, formed in cumulonimbus clouds. (p. D76)

tissue (tish′ü) A group of similar cells that work together at the same job. (p. A8)

topsoil (top′soil′) The dark, top layer of soil, rich in humus and minerals, in which many tiny organisms live and most plants grow. (p. B9)

tornado (tôr nā′dō) A violent, whirling wind that moves across the ground in a narrow path. (p. D77)

trade wind (trād wind) A belt of winds around Earth moving from high pressure zones toward the low pressure at the equator. (p. D58)

translucent (trans lü′sənt) Letting only some light through, so that objects on the other side appear blurry. (p. F96)

transparent (trans pâr′ənt) Letting all light through, so that objects on the other side can be seen clearly. (p. F96)

transpiration (tran′spə rā′shən) The loss of water through a plant's leaves. (pp. A35, A38, D39)

trench (trench) A deep valley in the sea floor. (p. C91)

tropical rain forest (trop′i kəl rān fôr′ist) A hot biome near the equator, with much rainfall and a wide variety of life. (p. B71)

tropism (trō′piz′əm) A response of a plant toward or away from a stimulus. (p. A44)

PRONUNCIATION KEY

a at; ā ape; ä far; âr care; ô law; e end; ē me; i it; ī ice; îr pierce; o hot; ō old; ôr fork; oi oil; ou out; u up; ū use; ü rule; ů pull; ûr turn; hw white; ng song; th thin; <u>th</u> this; zh measure; ə about, taken, pencil, lemon, circus

troposphere (trop′ə sfîr′) The layer of the atmosphere closest to Earth's surface. (p. D32)

tube worm (tüb wûrm) Large wormlike animals that live near sea-floor vents and obtain their food through bacterial chemosynthesis. (p. C93)

tundra (tun′dra) Large, treeless plain in the arctic regions, where the ground is frozen all year. (p. B68)

U

ultrasonic (ul′trə son′ik) Said of a sound with a frequency too high to be heard by humans. (p. F57)

unbalanced forces (un bal′ənst fôrs′əz) Forces that do not cancel each other out when acting together on a single object. (p. F21)

updraft (up′draft′) An upward rush of heated air during a thunderstorm. (pp. D55, D76)

V

vacuum (vak′ū əm) A space through which sound waves cannot travel because it contains no matter. (p. F116)

valley breeze (val′ē brēz) A cool wind that blows up a mountain slope and replaces the slope's rising Sun-warmed air. (p. D56)

variable (vâr′ē ə bəl) One of the changes in a situation that may affect the outcome of an experiment. (p. A48)

vascular (vas′kyə lər) Containing plant tissue through which water moves up and food moves down. (p. A15)

velocity (və los′i tē) The speed and direction of a moving object. (p. F12)

vertebrate (vûr′tə brit) An animal that has a backbone. (p. A16)

vibration (vī brā′shən) A back-and-forth motion. (p. F50)

volume (vol′ūm) **1.** A measure of how much space an object takes up. (p. E6) **2.** The loudness or softness of a sound. (p. F58)

W

warm front (wôrm frunt) A front where warm air moves in over a cold air mass. (p. D72)

water cycle (wô′tər sī′kəl) The continuous movement of water between Earth's surface and the air, changing from liquid to gas to liquid. (pp. B51, C74)

water table (wô′tər tā′bəl) The top of the water-filled spaces in the ground. (p. C75)

water vapor (wô′tər vā′pər) Water in the form of a gas. (pp. B50, D38)

watershed (wô′tər shed′) Area from which water is drained; region that contributes water to a river or river system. (pp. C20, C68–C69)

weather (we<u>th</u>′ər) What the lower atmosphere is like at any given place and time. (p. D34)

weathering (we<u>th</u>′ər ing) Breaking down rocks into smaller pieces. (p. C10)

weight (wāt) The force of gravity between Earth and an object. (pp. E7, F36)

well (wel) A hole dug below the water table that water seeps into. (p. C75)

wind (wind) Air that moves horizontally. (p. D55)

work (wûrk) The use of force to move an object a certain distance. (p. F26)

X

xylem (zī′ləm) The tissue through which water and minerals move up through a plant. (pp. A30, A32)

Y

year (yîr) The time it takes a planet to orbit the Sun. A *year* is different from planet to planet. (p. D7)

Index

A

Abiotic factors, B6–7
Absorption, of sound, F66–67
Abyssal plain, C90
Acceleration, F13, F18–20
  calculation of, F20
  of falling objects, F36–37
  force and, F18
  importance of understanding, F29
  mass and, F19, F20
  of the Moon, F37
Acid rain, C11, C65, C81
Acidity, E86–87
Acids, C65*
  identifying, E81*–82, E84–85
  importance of understanding, E89
  reaction with bases, E82–83
  reactivity of, E83
  strength of, E86–87
  uses of, E88
Action, F24
Adaptation, A42–51, A46, A104–120
  camouflage as, A108–109
  competition as, A47, B23
  mimicry as, A106–107
  root growth as, A43*
  in sowbugs, A105*
  in taste, A107
  thorns as, A107
  tropisms, A44–45
Aerial roots, A31
Aerogels, E16
Aerosol, E60
African violets, A86
Agnatha, A98
Agriculture, B76–77
Air
  cleaning up, C66
  composition of, D33
  cooling of, D40
  dirty, C61*
  dust in, D33

nitrogen in, B54
  pollution of, C64, C67
  as solution, E56
  water in, D39
Air masses, D70–71, D78
Air pollution, B38
Air pressure
  altitude and, D33
  changes in, D53*–54
  convection cells and, D55
  hurricane formation and, D78–79
  isobars, D59
  measuring, D34
  storm surges and, D79
Air resistance, F34
Air sac (swim bladder), A98
Air temperature
  altitude and, D32
  importance of understanding, D35
  measuring, D34
  relative humidity and, D39
  Sun's angle and, D29*–31*
Algae, B28, B73
  blooms, B30
  green, A18, A64
  as producers, B7
Alkalinity, E86–87
Alloys, E56
Alternation of generations, A63
Alternative energy sources, C104–105, C106
Altitude
  air pressure and, D33, D54
  air temperature and, D32
  climate and, D87
Altocumulus clouds, D45
Altostratus clouds, D45
Aluminum, C38, E23
Alvin (submersible), C92–93
AM, F120
Amazing Stories
  coral reefs, B42–43
  icy survival, E18–19
  milk vs. butter, E66–67
  planetary weather, D22–23

weightlessness, F42–43
Ammeter, E93
Ammonia, B54, B56, E83
Amperes, E93
Amphibia, A95, A98
Amphibians, A16
Amplifier, F60
Anaconda, B71
"Ancient" bacteria kingdom, A19
Anemometer, D62
Anemones, A16, A96
Aneroid barometer, D34
Angiosperms, A15, A64, A68, A69, A71–75
  aromatic flowers, A84
  cotyledons, A72–73, A82
  importance of understanding, A75, A85
  life cycle of, A74
Animals, A16, A90–120. See also Populations
  adaptation of, A104–120
    camouflage, A108–109
    mimicry, A106–107
    sowbugs, A105*
    taste, A107
    thornbugs, A107
  carbon cycle and, B53
  classification of, A16
    importance of understanding, A21
  as consumers, B7
  crossbreeds, A112–113
  in deciduous forests, B70
  diversity among, A114
  habitat change and, B13*, B36
  hoofed, B66
  hybrids, A112*
  importance of understanding, A101, A115
  inherited vs. learned traits in, A110–111
  invertebrates, A95, A96–97
  life cycles of, A102–103
  in nitrogen cycle, B55
  plants vs., A16
  in prairie ecosystem, B10

* Indicates an activity related to this topic.

*Indicates an activity related to this topic.

*Indicates an activity related to this topic.

*Indicates an activity related to this topic.

*Indicates an activity related to this topic.

*Indicates an activity related to this topic.

*Indicates an activity related to this topic.

*Indicates an activity related to this topic.

Woody stem, A32
Work, F26
    energy and, E94
    simple machines to do, F26

X rays, F121
Xylem, A30, A32, A39

Yeasts, A17
Yellow, F112, F113
Yellow jackets, A106
Yucca moths, B25
Yucca plant (Joshua tree), B25

Credits

Cover Photos: Chris Johns/National Geographic; bkgd. ThinkStock/Superstock.

Photography Credits: All photographs are by Macmillan/McGraw-Hill (MMH) except as noted below:

Unit A: A0 (bkgd) Kelvin Aitken/Peter Arnold Inc; A1 (bkgd) Norbert Wu/Norbert Wu; A1 (br) Kelvin Aitken/Peter Arnold Inc; A2-A3 (bkgd) Gallo Images/Corbis; A4 (bkgd) Ted Levin/Animals Animals/Earth Scenes; A5 (r) Richard Hutchings for MMH; A6 (bl) Peter Miller/Photo Researchers, Inc.; A7 (br) Dick Thomas/Visuals Unlimited; A9 (b) Rob Hadlow/Bruce Coleman, Inc.; A12 Carol Cohen/Corbis; A13 (br) Ken Karp for MMH; A17 (bc) Doug Sokell/Visuals Unlimited; A17 (bcl) Veronika Burmeister/Visuals Unlimited; A17 (bcr) R.M. Meadows/Peter Arnold, Inc.; A18 (bc) Veronika Burmeister/Visuals Unlimited; A18 (bcl) Patrick W. Grace/Science Source/Photo Researchers, Inc.; A18 (bcr) Cabisco/Visuals Unlimited; A18 (bl) Gilbert S. Grant/Photo Researchers, Inc.; A18 (br) R. Kessel-G. Shih/Visuals Unlimited; A19 (bcl) Telegraph Colour Library/FPG/Getty Images; A19 (bcr) A. & F. Michler/Peter Arnold, Inc.; A19 (bl) R. Robinson/Visuals Unlimited; A20 (b) Jim Roetzel/Dembinsky Photo Associates; A20 (bc) Skip Moody/Dembinsky Photo Associates; A20 (br) John Shaw/Bruce Coleman, Inc.; A20 (c) John Cancalosi/Peter Arnold, Inc.; A20 (cr) E.R. Degginger/Color-Pic, Inc.; A21 (cr) Manfred Kage/Peter Arnold, Inc.; A25 (cl) Hans Reinhard/Bruce Coleman, Inc.; A26 (bkgd) William Waterfall/The Stock Market; A28-9 (bkgd) Dominique Braud/Dembinsky Photo Associates; A29 (br) Richard Hutchings for MMH; A33 (b) Willard Clay/Dembinsky Photo Associates; A33 (tl) George Bernard/Animals Animals/Earth Scenes; A33 (tr) ©Robert Maier/Animals Animals/Earth Scenes; A36 (t) PHOTODISC/Getty Images; A38 (bl) Jack M. Bostrack/Visuals Unlimited; A38 (br) Jack M. Bostrack/Visuals Unlimited; A38 (t) Gerry Ellis/ENP Images; A39 (tl) Phil Degginger/Color-Pic, Inc.; A41 (cr) James R. Holland/National Geographic Society; A42-A43 Kalpana Kartik/Alamy Images; A44 (b) David Newman/Visuals Unlimited; A45 (tr) R. Calentine/Visuals Unlimited; A47 (b) Bill Beatty/Visuals Unlimited; A47 (tr) Parke H. John, Jr./Visuals Unlimited; A49 Royalty-Free/CORBIS; A50-1 (bkgd) Jim Olive/Pictor/Uniphoto; A51 (cr) WHM Bildarchiv/Peter Arnold, Inc.; A51 (tcr) Hans Reinhard/Bruce Coleman, Inc.; A51 (tl) Prof. K. Banks/©courtesy of Katherine Banks; A53 (cl) David Newman/Visuals Unlimited; A54 (bkgd) Bob Krist/CORBIS; A56-7 (bkgd) ©Michael Fogden/Bruce Coleman, Inc.; A57 (br) Richard Hutchings for MMH; A58 (bcl) John Trager/Visuals Unlimited; A58 (bcr) David Sieren/Visuals Unlimited; A58 (cl) Doug Sokell/Visuals Unlimited; A59 (bcl) Ed Reschke/Peter Arnold, Inc.; A59 (c) Mike Perry/Pictor/Uniphoto; A60 (b) Richard Hutchings for MMH; A60 (t) Richard Hutchings for MMH; A61 David Dennis/Animals Animals/Earth Scenes; A64 (tcr) Dick Keen/Visuals Unlimited; A65 (tc) E.R. Degginger/Color-Pic, Inc.; A66-7 (bkgd) Michael Gadomski/Animals Animals/Earth Scenes; A67 (br) Richard Hutchings for MMH; A68 (bl) Jim Hughes/Visuals Unlimited; A68 (br) V.P. Weinland/Photo Researchers, Inc.; A68 (c) W. Ormerod/Visuals Unlimited; A69 (bc) Gerald & Buff Corsi/Visuals Unlimited; A69 (br) E. Webber/Visuals Unlimited; A69 (inset) John N. Trager/Visuals Unlimited; A69 (l) Jan Taylor/Bruce Coleman, Inc.; A69 (r) E.R. Degginger/Bruce Coleman, Inc.; A70 (tl) Scott T. Smith/CORBIS; A71 (b) V. McMillan/Visuals Unlimited; A71 (t) E.F. Anderson/Visuals Unlimited; A73 (b) Visuals Unlimited/©Arthur R. Hill/VU; A73 (r) Mark S. Skalny/Visuals Unlimited; A74 (tl) SIME s.a.s./E-stock Photo; A75 (r) PhotoDisc; A76-7 (bkgd) Robert P. Carr/Bruce Coleman, Inc.; A77 (br) Richard Hutchings for MMH; A79 (b) Adam Jones/Photo Researchers, Inc.; A79 (cl) Doug Sokell/Visuals Unlimited; A79 (tl) Derrick Ditchburn/Visuals Unlimited; A82 (b) Henry T. Kaiser/Pictor/Uniphoto; A83 (cr) Stephen J. Lang/Visuals Unlimited; A83 (tc) Inga Spence/Visuals Unlimited; A83 (tr) Ken Wagner/Visuals Unlimited; A84 (tc) Jerome Wexler/Photo Researchers, Inc.; A84 (tl) John Gerlach/Visuals Unlimited; A89 (bl) Hans Reinhard/Bruce Coleman, Inc.; cl) John McAnulty/CORBIS; A90-1 (bkgd) R&V Taylor/Bruce Coleman, Inc.; A92-A93 ABPL/HAAGNER, CLEM/Animals Animals; A94 (b) ZEFA/Rauschenbach/Masterfile; A94 (t) Fred Bavendam/Minden Pictures; A95 (bl) BIOS Klein/Hubert/Peter Arnold, Inc.; A95 (tr) Joe McDonald/Bruce Coleman, Inc.; A96 (bcl) Tom E. Adams/Peter Arnold, Inc.; A96 (br) E.R. Degginger/Color-Pic, Inc.; A96 (cr) Scott Johnson/Animals Animals/Earth Scenes; A96 (tc) Jeff Mondragon/Mondragon Photography; A96 (tcr) E.R. Degginger/Color-Pic, Inc.; A96 (tl) Susan Blanchet/Dembinsky Photo Associates; A97 (bcl) Breck P. Kent/Animals Animals/Earth Scenes; A97 (bl) Pictor/Uniphoto; A97 (br) Fred Bavendam/Peter Arnold, Inc.; A97 (c) Robert Lubeck/Animals Animals/Earth Scenes; A97 (cl) Jeff J. Daly/Stock Boston; A97 (cr) Fred Bavendam/Peter Arnold, Inc.; A97 (t) Hans Pfletschinger/Peter Arnold, Inc.; A98 (bcl) Norbert Wu/Peter Arnold, Inc.; A98 (bl) Skip Moody/Dembinsky Photo Associates; A98 (br) Gary Meszaros/Bruce Coleman, Inc.; A98 (cr) Marilyn Kazmers/Dembinsky Photo Associates; A98 (tcr) UNIPHOTO, Inc./Pictor/Uniphoto; A98 (tl) Zig Leszczynski/Animals Animals/Earth Scenes; A99 (bcr) Bob Cranston/Animals Animals/Earth Scenes; A99 (br) Rob Simpson/Pictor/Uniphoto; A99 (c) Des & Jen Bartlett/Bruce Coleman, Inc.; A99 (cl) E.R. Degginger/Color-Pic, Inc.; A99 (tc) Michael Newman/PhotoEdit; A99 (tcl) Darrell Gulin/CORBIS; A99 (tr) UNIPHOTO, Inc./Pictor/Uniphoto; A100 (b) Ken Karp for MMH; A101 (c) Graham Pizzey/Bruce Coleman, Inc.; A104 (bkgd) John Gerlach/Dembinsky Photo Associates; A104 (inset) Rolf Kopfle/Bruce Coleman, Inc.; A105 (A106 (bl) L. West/Bruce Coleman, Inc.; A106 (br) Stan W. Elems/Visuals Unlimited; A106 (tr) Visuals Unlimited/©Stan W. Elems/VU; A107 (bl) E.R. Degginger/Color-Pic, Inc.; A107 (cl) Visuals Unlimited/©Stan W. Elems/VU; A107 (cr) Rod Planck/Dembinsky Photo Associates; A108 (b) Steve Kaufman/Peter Arnold, Inc.; A109 (t) Kim Taylor/Bruce Coleman, Inc.; A110 (tl) E.R. Degginger/Color-Pic, Inc.; A110 (tr) E.R. Degginger/Color-Pic, Inc.; A110-1 (b) D. Robert Franz/Bruce Coleman, Inc.; A111 (br) Erwin & Peggy Bauer/Bruce Coleman, Inc.; A111 (tc) John Shaw/Bruce Coleman, Inc.; A111 (tl) John Snyder/Bruce Coleman, Inc.; A111 (tr) Skip Moody/Dembinsky Photo Associates; A112 (cl) E.R. Degginger/Color-Pic, Inc.; A112 (tc) E.R. Degginger/Color-Pic, Inc.; A112 (tl) Randa Bishop/Pictor/Uniphoto; A113 (bc) Image Bank/Getty Images; A113 (bl) Akira Matoba; A113 (br) Shoot Photography/Image State; A114 (b) Stan Osolinski/Dembinsky Photo Associates; A115 (tcr) Gerard Lacz/Animals Animals/Earth Scenes; A117 (tcl) Stan W. Elems/Visuals Unlimited; A19 (br) Blair Seitz/Photo Researchers, Inc.; A59 (cr) E.F.Anderson/Visuals Unlimited.

Unit B: B0-1 (bkgd) Art Wolfe/Stone; B1 (br) Tim Flach/Stone; B2-3 (bkgd) Lee Rentz/Bruce Coleman, Inc.; B4-5 (bkgd) Zig Leszczynski/Animals Animals/Earth Scenes; B5 (br) Richard Hutchings for MMH; B8 (b) John Shaw/Bruce Coleman, Inc.; B8-9 (t) John Shaw/Bruce Coleman, Inc.; B0 (bkgd) Tim Flach/Stone; B10 (cl) John Giustina/Bruce Coleman, Inc.; B10 (cr) Joe McDonald/CORBIS; B10 (t) David J. Sams/Stock Boston; B11 (b) Lee Rentz/Bruce Coleman, Inc.; B12 (b) Robert M. Balou/Animals Animals/Earth Scenes; B12 (t) Laura Riley/Bruce Coleman, Inc.; B13 (b) PhotoDisc/Getty Images; B14 (b) James Carmichael/Bruce Coleman, Inc.; B22 (b) Joe McDonald/Bruce Coleman, Inc.; B22 (cl) Larry West/ Bruce Coleman Inc; B22 (cr) Gary Braasch/Stone/Getty Images; B23 (bl) Scott Smith/Animals Animals; B23 (tr) Doug Wechsler/Animals Animals; B24 (t) M.P.L. Fogden/Bruce Coleman, Inc.; B24-5 (b) Mark Newman/Bruce Coleman, Inc.; B26 (bcl) E.R. Degginger/ Animals Animals; B26 (bl) Image Club; B26 (br) John Shaw/Bruce Coleman, Inc.; B26 (tr) David Overcash/Bruce Coleman, Inc.; B27 (bl) Patty Murray/Earth Scenes; B27 (t) Lawrence Naylor/Photo Researchers; B30 (c) John Pontier/Animals Animals; B30 (t) Jeff Foote/Bruce Coleman, Inc.; B32-3 (bkgd) James Randklev/Stone/Getty Images; B33 (br) Richard Hutchings for MMH; B34 (bl) John Shaw/Bruce Coleman, Inc.; B34 (br) B&C Calhoun/Bruce Coleman, Inc.; B35 (b) Jeff Foott/Bruce Coleman, Inc.; B36 (tr) N.E. Swedberg/Bruce Coleman, Inc.; B37 (br) Joe McDonald/Animals Animals/Earth Scenes; B38 (tr) Buddy Mays/Corbis; B39 (bl) Steve Dunwell/Index Stock; B39 (t) Creation Captured/Index Stock; B40 (t) John H. Hoffman/Bruce Coleman, Inc.; B42 (t) Lynn Funkhouser/Peter Arnold, Inc.; B42-3 (bkgd) Joe Sroka/Dembinsky Photo Associates; B43 (cl) Kelvin Aitken/Peter Arnold, Inc.; B43 (cr) Fred Bavendam/Peter Arnold, Inc.; B46-7 (bkgd) Kennan Ward/The Stock Market/CORBIS; B48-9 (bkgd) John Shaw/Bruce Coleman, Inc.; B49 (br) Richard Hutchings for MMH; B56 (t) E.R. Degginger/Earth Scenes; B57 (bc) Cesar Llacuna for MMH; B57 (bl) Cesar Llacuna for MMH; B59 (tcr) Peter Beck/The Stock Market/CORBIS; B62-3 (bkgd) UNIPHOTO, Inc./Pictor; B63 (br) Richard Hutchings for MMH; B64 (c) Nigel J.H. Smith/Earth Scenes; B64 (t) Breck P. Kent/Earth Scenes; B64 (tc) Lee Rentz/Rentl/Bruce Coleman, Inc.; B65 (br) M. Timothy O'Keefe/Bruce Coleman, Inc.; B65 (tl) J.C. Carton/Bruce Coleman, Inc.; B65 (tr) Eastcott/Momatiuk/Earth Scenes; B66 (t) A.&M. Shah/Animals Animals; B67 (b) Eastcott/Momatiuk/Earth Scenes; B68 (t) Joe McDonald/Bruce Coleman, Inc.; B68-9 (c) Joy Spurr/Bruce Coleman, Inc.; B69 (bl) Jen & Des Bartlett/Bruce Coleman, Inc.; B70 (bl) Jeff Foott/Bruce Coleman, Inc.; B70 (cr) John Shaw/Bruce Coleman, Inc.; B71 (br) E&P Bauer/Bruce Coleman, Inc.; B71 (tr) Joe McDonald/CORBIS; B72 (bl) PhotoDisc/Getty Images; B74 (t) M. Newman/Bruce Coleman, Inc.; B78-9 (bkgd) Gary Braasch/CORBIS; B79 (br) Danny Lehman/CORBIS; B80 (tr) John Elk III/Bruce Coleman, Inc.; B82 (bl) The Image Bank/Getty Images. B82 (br) David Falconer/Bruce Coleman, Inc. B83 (bl) John Lemker/Earth Scenes; B83 Gibson Stock Photography; B85 (l) E.R. Degginger/Earth Scenes; B85 (r) PhotoDisc/Getty Images; B86 (b) E.R. Degginger/Earth Scenes; B86 (r) S. Jonasson/Bruce Coleman, Inc.; B87 (br) Richard Hutchings for MMH; B88 (t) Tom Bean/CORBIS; B88-9 (b) Bob Burch/Bruce Coleman, Inc.; B91 (b) John Elk III/Bruce Coleman, Inc.;

B16-7 (bkgd) Beverly Joubert/National Geographic Collection/GettyOne Images.

Unit C: C0 (bkgd) Jules Cowan/Index Stock Imagery; C1 (bkgd) Jules Cowan/Index Stock Imagery; C2-3 (bkgd) Peter French/Bruce Coleman, Inc.; C4-5 (bkgd) AFB/CORBIS; C5 (br) Richard Hutchings for MMH; C6 (b) John D. Cunningham/Visuals Unlimited; C6 (inset) Sinclair Stammers/Science Photo Library/Photo Researchers, Inc.; C9 (bl) Dr. E.R. Degginger/Color-Pic, Inc.; C9 (tr) Stella Snead/Bruce Coleman, Inc.; C10 (bl) Jerry Schad/Photo Researchers, Inc.; C10 (br) Jim Steinberg/Photo Researchers, Inc.; C10 (tr) ©Jeff Greenberg/Index Stock Imagery; C11 (bl) Gilbert Grant/Photo Researchers, Inc.; C11 (tr) ©Zandria Muench Beraldo/CORBIS; C12 (b) Renee Lynn/Photo Researchers, Inc.; C13 (t) Terranova International/Photo Researchers, Inc.; C14 (b) Detlev van Ravenswaay/Photo Researchers, Inc.; C14 (c) John Chumack/PRI; C14 (t) NASA/PhotoTake; C18-9 (bkgd) ©Walter Bibikow/Index Stock Imagery; C20 (b) ©Jim Wark/Index Stock Imagery; C20 (tr) ©Mick Roessler/Index Stock Imagery; C21 (t) Yann Arthus-Bertrand/Corbis; C22 (b) Bob Krist/Corbis; C22 (cr) ©Jules Cowan/Index Stock Imagery; C23 (tl) ©Diaphor Agency/Index Stock Imagery; C24 (tr) NASA/Goddard Space Flight Center, The SeaWiFs Project and ORBIMAGE, Scientific Visualization Studio; C26 (r) NASA/NASA; C27 (tr) Randy Faris/Corbis; C28 (b) Mark Mellett/Stock, Boston; C28-9 (b) Dave Bartruff/Stock, Boston; C29 (tl) Annie Griffiths Belt/Bettmann/Corbis; C29 (tr) Morton Beebe,S.F./Bettmann/Corbis; C30-1 (bkgd) George Lepp/CORBIS; C32 (bc) Charles D. Winters/Timeframe Photography Inc./Photo Researchers, Inc.; C32 (bcl) Cesar Llacuna for MMH; C32 (bcr) Function Thru Form; C32 (c) Joyce Photographics/Photo Researchers, Inc.; C32 (cl) E. R. Degginger/Photo Researchers, Inc.; C32 (cr) George Whiteley/Photo Researchers, Inc.; C33 (bc) Cesar Llacuna for MMH; C33 (bcl) David Lees/CORBIS; C33 (bcr) Cesar Llacuna for MMH; C33 (c) Kaj R. Svensson/Science Photo Library/Photo Researchers, Inc.; C33 (cl) Roberto De Gugliemo/Science Photo Library/Photo Researchers, Inc.; C33 (cr) J.H. Robinson/Photo Researchers, Inc.; C34 (tc) Mark A. Schneider/Visuals Unlimited; C34 (tl) John D. Cunningham/Visuals Unlimited; C34 (tr) Tom Pantages/PhotoTake; C35 (tl) A.J. Cunningham/Visuals Unlimited; C36 (bl) Ross Frid/Korner Gems, Traverse City, MI/Visuals Unlimited; C36 (br) Charles O'Rear/CORBIS; C36 (c) Joyce Photographics/Photo Researchers, Inc.; C36 (tr) A.J.Copley/Visuals Unlimited; C37 (tl) Peter Aitken/Photo Researchers, Inc.; C38 (bcl) A.J. Copley/Visuals Unlimited; C38 (bl) David Young-Wolff/PhotoEdit/PictureQuest; C38 (cr) Color Image/SuperStock; C38 (t) Richard T. Nowitz/Photo Researchers, Inc.; C40-1 (bkgd) Lee Rentz/Bruce Coleman, Inc.; C41 (br) Richard Hutchings for MMH; C42 (bc) Doug Sokell/Visuals Unlimited; C42 (bl) Andrew J. Martinez/Photo Researchers, Inc.; C42 (br) Andrew J. Martinez/Photo Researchers, Inc.; C43 (bl) E.R. Degginger/Photo Researchers, Inc.; C43 (br) AJ Copley/Visuals Unlimited; C44 (bcr) Joyce Photographics/Photo Researchers, Inc.; C44 (bl) Andrew J. Martinez/Photo Researchers, Inc.; C44 (br) Visuals Unlimited/©A.J. Copley/VU; C44 (tcr) Martin G. Miller/Visuals Unlimited; C44 (tr) Andrew J. Martinez/Photo Researchers, Inc.; C45 (b) John D. Cunningham/Visuals Unlimited; C45 (bl) Joyce Photographics/Photo Researchers, Inc.; C45 (cl) Kjell B. Sandved/Photo Researchers, Inc.; C46 (bl) E.R. Degginger/Photo Researchers, Inc.; C46 (br) Charles R. Belinky /Photo Researchers, Inc.; C46 (tl) Arthur R. Hill/Visuals Unlimited; C46 (tr) L.S. Stepanowicz/Visuals Unlimited; C47 (c) Michael P. Gadomski/Photo Researchers, Inc.; C48 (br) Joyce Photographics/Photo Researchers, Inc.; C48 (inset) Joyce Photographics/Photo Researchers, Inc.; C50 (bl) G. Büttner/Naturbild/OKAPIA/Photo Researchers, Inc.; C51 (tl) Ron Spomer/Visuals Unlimited; C53 (cr) John Elk III/Stock, Boston; C57 (cr) Detlev van Ravenswaay/Photo Researchers; C58-9 (bkgd) Paul Steel/The Stock Market/CORBIS; C60-1 (bkgd) NASA; C61 (br) Richard Hutchings for MMH; C62 (bl) Photodisc/Getty Images; C64 (br) Hattie Young/Science Photo Library/Photo Researchers, Inc.; C64 (tl) Phil Degginger/Color-Pic, Inc.; C64 (tr) Gary Withey/Bruce Coleman, Inc.; C65 (b) Simon Fraser/Science Photo Library/Photo Researchers, Inc.; C67 (br) Chase Swift/Corbis; C67 (tr) McGraw-Hill School Division/; C70-1 (bkgd) IFA/Peter Arnold, Inc.; C71 (tr) Richard Hutchings for MMH; C73 (t) Calvin Larsen/Photo Researchers, Inc.; C76 (b) Simon Fraser/Science Photo Library/Photo Researchers, Inc.; C77 (br) Richard Hutchings for MMH; C82-3 (bkgd) Dave G. Houser/PICTOR/Image State; C84 (tc) L.Lipsky/Bruce Coleman, Inc.; C84-5 (t) VCG/FPG/Getty Images; C85 (tc) Jan Stromme/Bruce Coleman, Inc.; C86 (cr) NASA/Tom Pantages; C87 (t) Ira Rubin/Dembinsky Photo Associates; C88 (b) Jeff Greenberg/PhotoEdit; C92 (b) Emory Kristof/National Geographic/Getty Images; C92 (tr) R&V Taylor/Bruce Coleman, Inc.; C93 (tr) Norbert Wu/Norbert Wu Productions; C94 (br) Fulvio Eccardi/Bruce Coleman, Inc.; C94 (t) Chinch Gryniewicz; Ecoscene/CORBIS; C95 (cr) PhotoDisc; C98-9 (bkgd) Ron Sherman/Stock Boston; C99 (br) Richard Hutchings for MMH; C100 (bl) Phil Degginger/Color-Pic, Inc.; C100 (br) Joseph Nettis/Photo Researchers, Inc.; C101 (t) Ted Speigel/Bettmann/CORBIS; C104 (bl) Simon Fraser/Science Photo Library/Photo Researchers, Inc.; C104 (tr) Phil Degginger/Color-Pic, Inc.;

C104-5 (b) Russell D. Curtis/Photo Researchers, Inc.; C105 (br) Kevin Schafer/Peter Arnold, Inc.; C105 (tl) John Keating/Photo Researchers, Inc.; C106 (tl) Patrick Grace/Peter Arnold, Inc.; C107 (cr) Matt Meadows/Peter Arnold, Inc.; C109 (tr) John Keating/Photo Researchers, Inc.

Unit D: D0 (bkgd) NOAA, colored by John Wells/Science Photo Library/Photo Researchers Inc; D1 (bkgd) World Perspectives/Stone; D2-3 Courtesy NASA/JPL-CalTech; D4 STSI/Photo Researchers Inc; D5 (br) Richard Hutchings for MMH; D7 (cl) Richard Hutchings for MMH; D10 (b) Science VU/Visuals Unlimited; D12 (tr) Pekka Parviainen/Dembinsky Photo Associates; D13 (cr) E.Karkoschka (Univ. of Az.) /NASA; D14 Courtesy NASA/ JPL-CalTech; D16 USGS/Photo Researchers, Inc.; D16 NASA/Science Source/Photo Researchers, Inc.; D16 USGS /Photo Researchers, Inc.; D18 (l) NASA/Photo Researchers, Inc.; D19 (l) NASA and Erich Karkoschka, University of Arizona; D19 (r) NASA/Phototake/Alamy Images; D20 (r) Ron Russell/Index Stock; D22 (bkgd) n/a; D22 (br) JPL/NASA; D23 (tl) NASA; D23 (tr) Photo Researchers, Inc.; D25 (bl) Ron Russell/Index Stock; D26 (bkgd) Steve Terrill/The Stock Market/CORBIS; D28 (bkgd) G.L. Kooyman/Animals Animals/Earth Scenes; D28 (br) Price, R. -Surv. OSF/Animals Animals/Earth Scenes; D29 (br) Richard Hutchings for MMH; D34 (tcl) Runk/Schoenberger/Grant Heilman Photography, Inc.; D34 (tr) Yoav Levy/PhotoTake; D35 (br) E.R. Degginger/Color-Pic, Inc.; D36 (bkgd) Wolfgang Kaehler/CORBIS; D37 (b) Richard Hutchings for MMH; D42 (bkgd) Bonnie Kamin/PhotoEdit; D43 (b) Richard Hutchings Photography/Richard Hutchings; D44 (br) Visuals Unlimited/©Mark A. Schneider/VU; D44 (cr) Visuals Unlimited/©Henry W. Robison/VU; D44 (tr) Visuals Unlimited/©A.J. Copley/VU; D46 (bcr) Visuals Unlimited/©Mark E. Gibson/VU; D46 (bl) Visuals Unlimited/©D. Cavagnaro/VU; D46 (bcl) Visuals Unlimited/©W. Banaszewski/VU; D46 (br) Corbis/Corbis/Bettmann; D47 (br) Dembinsky Photo Associates/©Michael P. Gadomski; D47 (cr) Fundamental Photographs/©Jeff J. Daly; D49 (tr) McGraw-Hill School Division/; D51 (tl) Corbis/©Sean Sexton/COBBIS; D52 (bkgd) Corbis/©Vince Streano/CORBIS; D53 (br) Hutchings/Richard Hutchings; D55 (b) Superstock/©Superstock; D56 (t) The Stock Market/©TSM/Torleif Svensson; D58 (bl) NASA. (br) Hutchings/Richard Hutchings; D61 (tcr) Corbis/©Paul A. Souders/CORBIS; D61 (tr) McGraw-Hill School Division/; D66 (bkgd) Animals Animals/Earth Scenes/©Stephen Ingram; D68 (bkgd) Animals Animals/Earth Scenes/©Bertram G. Murray JR; D73 (tr) Animals Animals/Earth Scenes/©Charles Palek; D77 (cr) Richard Hutchings Photography/Richard Hutchings; D79 (b) Visuals Unlimited/©Science VU; D80 (bl) Peter Arnold, Inc./©NOAA/Peter Arnold, Inc.; D80 (br) Carlos Guerrero/Carlos Guerrero; D82 (bkgd) Animals Animals/Earth Scenes/©Arthur Gloor; D85 (br) Hutchings/Richard Hutchings; D87 Benelux Press/Index Stock; D88 (l) Visuals Unlimited/©Science VU; D88 (r) Visuals Unlimited/©VU; D89 Superstock; D90 (br) PhotoEdit/Jeff Greenberg; D90 (tr) Tony Stone Images/©Don Smetzer/TSI; D91 (cr) Bridgeman Art Library Int'l Ltd/Frost Fair on the Thames, Abraham Hondius, Museum of London, UK, The Bridgeman Art Library D93 (bcl) Dembinsky Photo Associates/©Mark A. Schneider;

Unit E: E0 (bkgd) Roger Ressmeyer/CORBIS; E2-E3 (bkgd) ©Christine Osborne/CORBIS; E4-E5 (bkgd) ©Michael T. Sedam/CORBIS; E5 (br) Richard Hutchings; E6 (b) Ken Karp/McGraw-Hill School Division; E8 (bl) ©Ken Karp/McGraw-Hill School Division; E8 (br) ©Ken Karp/McGraw-Hill School Division; E8 (c) Ken Karp/McGraw-Hill School Division; E9 (br) Richard Hutchings; E11 (bcr) Wolfgang Kaehler/Bettman/CORBIS; E11 (bl) Buddy Mays/Bettman/CORBIS; E11 (tc) George Bernard/Photo Researchers, Inc. (tr) /Klaus Guldbrandsen/ Science Photo Library/Photo Researchers, Inc.; E11 Sinclair Stammers/Science Photo Library/Photo Researchers; E11 Chris McElcheran/Masterfile; E13 (tr) ©Carl Purcell/Photo Researchers, Inc.; E14 (b) ©Kim Sayer/CORBIS; E14 (br) Phil Degginger/Color-Pic, Inc.; E14 (tr) Phil Degginger/Color-Pic, Inc.; E15 PhotoDisc; E16 (b) ©National Railway of Japan/ PhotoTake; E16 (cr) IBM Research/Peter Arnold, Inc.; E16 (tr) Lawrence Livermore National Laboratory/Science Photo Library/Photo Researchers, Inc.; E17 (bcr) McGraw-Hill School Division; E18 (bkgd) Rod Plack/Photo Researchers, Inc.; E20 (bkgd) Stock Trek/PhotoDisc; E21 Ken Karp for MMH; E22 (b) Lowell Georgia/Photo Researchers, Inc.; (tcr) Rich Treptow/Photo Researchers, Inc.; E23 (bcr) Charles D. Winters/Photo Researchers, Inc.; E23 (br) Charles D. Winters/Photo Researchers, Inc.; E23 (cr) Charles D. Winters/Photo Researchers, Inc.; E23 (cr) Russ Lappa/ Science Source/Photo Researchers, Inc.; E23 (tc) ©Science/VU/Visuals Unlimited; E23 (tr) Charles D. Winters/Photo Researchers, Inc.; E24 (bc) Yoav Levy/Phototake; E24 (bl) Bill Beatty/VU/Visuals Unlimited; E24 (br) 1998 Photodisc; E24 (cl) Charles D. Winters/Photo Researchers, Inc.; E25 (tc) David Taylor/Photo Researchers, Inc.; E25 (tl) David Taylor/Photo Researchers, Inc.; E25 (tr) David Taylor/Photo Researchers, Inc.; E26 ©Colin Cuthbert/Photo Researchers, Inc.; E28 (bcr) ©E.R. Degginger/Color-Pic, Inc.; E28 (bl) ©Charles D. Winters/Photo. Researchers, Inc.; E28 (br) Russ Lappa/Photo

Researchers, Inc.; E28 (c) Klaus Guldbrandsen/ Science Photo Library/Photo Researchers, Inc.; E28 (cl) George Bernard/Photo Researchers, Inc.; E28 (cr) Klaus Guldbrandsen/Science Photo Library/Photo Researchers, Inc.; E28 (tl) Dr. E. R. Degginger/Color-Pic, Inc.; E28 (tr) Dr. E. R. Degginger/Color-Pic, Inc.; E31 (tr) McGraw-Hill School Division; E32 (bl) Christine Coscioni/CO2, Inc.; E32 (cl) Christine Coscioni/CO2; E32 (tcr) Leonard Lessin/Peter Arnold, Inc.; E33 PhotoDisc; E34 (bkgd) ©W.Wisniewski/Okapia/Photo Researchers, Inc.; E35 Ken Karp for MMH; E36 (bc) Clyde H. Smith/Peter Arnold, Inc.; E36 (bl) Gordon Wiltsie/Peter Arnold, Inc.; E36 (br) Jeff & Alexa Henry/Peter Arnold, Inc.; E37 (cl) Cesar Llacuna/Cesar Llacuna; E37 (cr) Cesar Llacuna/Cesar Llacuna; E37 (tl) Cesar Llacuna/Cesar Llacuna; E40 (bcr) Charles D. Winters/Photo Researchers, Inc.; E40 (br) Charles D. Winters/Photo Researchers, Inc.; E40 (c) Christine L. Coscioni/CO2, Inc.; E40 (t) Cesar Llacuna/Cesar Llacuna; E40 (tcr) ©Carolina Biological Supply/PhotoTake; E41 (b) Richard Hutchings; E41 (tcr) n/a; E42 (bl) ©Jack Plekan/Fundamental Photographs; E42 (tr) Richard Choy/Peter Arnold, Inc.; E42 Image Port/Index Stock; E48 (bkgd) ©Paul A. Souders/CORBIS; E50 (bkgd) ©Nathan Benn/CORBIS; E51 (br) Richard Hutchings/Hutchings; E52 (bl) ©Charles D. Winters/Photo Researchers, Inc; E52 (br) Jacana/Photo Researchers, Inc.; E53 (br) ©Phil Degginger/Color-Pic, Inc.; E53 (c) ©Becky Luigart-Stayner/CORBIS; E53 (cl) ©Dr. Ed Degginger/Color-Pic, Inc.; E53 (tl) Dr. Ed Degginger/Color-Pic; E53 (tr) ©E.R. Degginger/Color-Pic, Inc.; E54 (bl) ©Phil Degginger/Color-Pic, Inc.; E54 (br) ©Phil Degginger/Color-Pic, Inc.; E54 (cr) Richard Hutchings/Hutchings; E55 (b) ©EyeWire/GETTYONE; E55 (bcr) ©Jim Corwin/Photo Researchers, Inc.; E55 (br) Phil Degginger/Color-Pic, Inc.; E55 (cr) Artville/Artville; E55 (t) ©Phil Degginger/Color-Pic, Inc.; E55 (tr) ©Phil Degginger/Color-Pic, Inc.; E56 (b) ©Phil Degginger/Color-Pic, Inc.; E56 (tr) Charles D. Winters/Photo Researchers, Inc.; E57 (tc) Richard Hutchings/Hutchings; E57 (tl) ©Richard Megna/Fundamental Photographs; E57 (tr) Richard Hutchings/Hutchings; E58 (bc) McGraw-Hill School Division; E59 (bl) Richard Hutchings/Hutchings; E59 (br) Richard Hutchings/Hutchings; E59 (tr) ©Joyce Photographics/Photo Researchers, Inc.; E60 (t) ©S. Strickland/Naturescapes/Visuals Unlimited; E61 (br) Richard Hutchings/Hutchings; E61 (cl) M.I. Walker/Photo Researchers, Inc.; E62 (bl) Hutchings/Richard Hutchings; E64 (b) ©Mark E. Gibson/VU/Visuals Unlimited; E65 (cr) ©Photodisc; E66 (c) Larry Lefever/Grant Heilman Photography, Inc.; E67 (l) David R. Frazier /Photo Researchers, Inc.; E67 (tr) ©David S. Addison/Visuals Unlimited; E68 (bkgd) ©Nik Wheeler/CORBIS; E70 (b) Richard Hutchings/Hutchings; E70 (br) Richard Hutchings/Hutchings; E70 (cr) Richard Hutchings/Hutchings; E70 (tc) Richard Hutchings/Hutchings; E70 (tr) ©Richard Hutchings/Richard Hutchings Photography; E71 (cr) Richard Hutchings/Hutchings; E72 (bl) ©Ed Degginger/Color-Pic, Inc.; E72 (br) Richard Hutchings/Hutchings; E73 (bl) ©Richard Megna/Fundamental Photographs; E73 (br) Lee Snyder/Photo Researchers, Inc.; E73 (tl) Richard Hutchings/Hutchings; E73 (tr) Richard Hutchings/Hutchings; E74 (tr) NASA; E74 (tl) Christine L. Coscioni/CO2, Inc.; E74 (tl) ©Science/Visuals Unlimited; E74 (tr) Leonard Lessin/Peter Arnold, Inc.; E74 (tr) Leonard Lessin/Peter Arnold, Inc.; E75 (br) Richard Hutchings/Richard Hutchings Photograph; E76 (bl) Christine Coscioni/CO2, Inc.; E76 (tr) Cesar Llacuna/Cesar Llacuna; E77 (tr) McGraw-Hill School Division; E78 (br) ©Henry Horenstein/Stock Boston; E79 (bkgd) ©LSF OSF/Animals Animals/Earth Scenes; E79 (tl) ©Michael Newman/PhotoEdit; E80 (bkgd) ©Michael P. Gadomski/Photo Researchers, Inc.; E81 (br) McGraw-Hill School Division; E82 (bcl) ©Ken Karp/Ken Karp Photography; E82 (bcr) PhotoDisc; E82 (bl) ©Richard Megna/Fundamental Photographs; E82 (br) ©E.R. Degginger/Color-Pic, Inc.; E83 (tr) ©Kristen Brochmann/Fundamental Photographs; E84 (bl) Geoff Bryant/Photo Researchers, Inc.; E84 (br) Ken Karp/McGraw Hill School Division; E84 (cl) ©John D. Cunningham/Visuals Unlimited; E85 (br) McGraw-Hill School Division; E85 (tl) ©Renee Lynn/Photo Researchers, Inc.; E87 (br) Dan Howell/McGraw-Hill School Division; E87 (cl) Dan Howell/McGraw-Hill School Division; E87 (tl) ©Dr. E.R. Degginger/Color-Pic, Inc.; E88 (l) ©Paul Silverman/Fundamental Photographs; E89 (r) Tony Freeman/PhotoEdit; E90 (bkgd) ©Denise Mattia/Denise Mattia Underwater Photography; E91 (br) Richard Hutchings/Hutchings; E93 (b) McGraw-Hill School Division; E96 (bl) Andrew McClenaghan/Photo Researchers, Inc.; E96 (br) ©Science/Visuals Unlimited; E97 (bc) ©Michael Dalton/Fundamental Photographs; E98 (cr) Richard Hutchings/Hutchings; E99 Bettmann/CORBIS; E101 (bl) Craig Lovell/Bettmann/CORBIS.

Unit F: F0 (bkgd) Comstock; F1 (bkgd) Duomo/CORBIS; F2 (bkgd) ©PHOTRI/Tom Sanders/ THE STOCK MARKET; F4-5 (bkgd) ©Annie Griffiths Belt/CORBIS; F5 (br) McGraw-Hill School Division; F5 (cr) McGraw-Hill School Division; F6 (b) McGraw-Hill School Division; F7 (tr) ©Paul Silverman/Fundamental Photographs; F8 (b) ©Neil Rabinowitz/CORBIS; F8 (inset) ©NASA/Ed Degginger/Color-Pic, Inc.; F9 (bcr) ©Duomo/Chris Trotman/Duomo Photography Inc.; F9 (bl) ©Joe McDonald/CORBIS; F9 (tl) Museum of Flight/CORBIS; F10 (c) ©Bill Aron/Photo Researchers, Inc.; F11 (tr) ©Jerry Wachter/Photo

Researchers, Inc.; F12 (tl) ©Peter Turnley/CORBIS; F13 (b) ©George Lepp/CORBIS; F13 (tr) ©Robert Mathena/Fundamental Photographs; F15 (cr) ©TSM/Photri/The Stock Market; F16-7 (bkgd) ©Ed Kashi/CORBIS; F17 (br) McGraw-Hill School Division; F17 (c) PhotoDisc/Getty Images; F17 (cr) PhotoDisc/Getty Images; F20 (tcr) ©Tony Freeman/PhotoEdit; F20 (tr) ©Ed Degginger/Color-Pic, Inc.; F21 (cr) ©Phil Degginger/Color-Pic, Inc.; F21 (tr) ©Ed Degginger/Color-Pic, Inc.; F22 (br) ©LBJ Space Center/Nasa/NASA; F25 (b) ©Kevin R. Morris/CORBIS; F25 (cl) ©Russ Schleipman/CORBIS; F25 (cr) ©Peter Turnley/CORBIS; F25 (tr) ©Paul A. Souders/CORBIS; F26 (bc) Eric Roth/FlashFocus; F26 (bl) Gregg Occo/Visuals Unlimited; F26 (br) StockByte; F26 (c) Larry Mulvehill/Photo Researchers, Inc.; F26 (cl) RDF/Visuals Unlimited; F26 (cr) Walley Eberhart/Visuals Unlimited; F29 (tr) McGraw-Hill School Division; F32 (bkgd) ©Bettmann/CORBIS; F33 (br) McGraw-Hill School Division; F35 (t) ©G.Sauvage/Vandystadt/Photo Researchers, Inc.; F36 (tr) ©J-L Charmet/Science Photo Library/Photo Researchers, Inc.; F40 (bl) ©Kevin R. Morris/Corbis; F40 (tl) ©The Image Bank/Gettyone; F40 (tr) ©Davis Barber/PhotoEdit; F41 (cr) ©NASA/Media Dallas; F42-3 (b) ©ZERO/JSC/NASA; F42-3 (bkgd) ©JSC/NASA; F45 (bcl) NASA/©Nasa; F46-7 (bkgd) ©Miro Vintoniv/Stock, Boston; F48-9 (bkgd) ©NASA/Galaxy Contact/Oxford Scientific Film and Photo Library; F49 (br) Richard Hutchings Photography/Richard Hutchings; F50 (bcl) Artville/Artville/PictureQuest, PhotoSpin; F50 (bcr) PictureQuest, PhotoSpin/Artville/Artville; F50 (bl) PictureQuest, PhotoSpin/Artville/Artville; F50 (br) Cartesia Software/Cartesia Software; F51 (bl) McGraw-Hill School Division; F52 (b) ©Ken Fisher/TSI/Tony Stone Images; F52 (c) PhotoDisc 2000; F53 (br) McGraw-Hill School Division; F54-5 (bkgd) ©Ulrike Welsch/Ulrike Welsch Photography; F55 (cr) Richard Hutchings/Hutchings; F56 (b) Artville LLC 1997/Artville; F56 (inset) Artville LLC 1997/Artville; F57 (t) Tim Davis/Photo Researchers, Inc.; F58 (bl) Courtesy Alexander Graham Bell/National Historic Park; F58 (tr) ©William James Warren/Corbis; F59 (tr) George Hall/CORBIS; F60 (t) ©1998 PhotoDisc, Inc.; F61 (c) Dr. Jeremy Burgess/Photo Researchers, Inc.; F62-3 (bkgd) Brenda Tharp/Photo Researchers, Inc.; F64-5 (bkgd) ©Kevin Fleming/CORBIS; F65 (br) Richard Hutchings/Hutchings; F66 (bl) ©Duomo/CORBIS; F66 (br) Brian Bahr/Allsport; F67 (b) ©Museum der Stadt, Vienna, Austria/Superstock; F67 (t) ©Marty Loken/Tony Stone Images/Stone; F68 (br) ©TSM/John M. Roberts/The Stock Market; F68 (cl) McGraw-Hill School Division; F69 (b) Wolfgang Kaehler/CORBIS; F72 (b) Joseph Schuyler/Stock, Boston; F72 (t) Artville; F73 (cr) Luc Novovitch/Gamma Liaison Agency; F77 (cr) PictureQuest, PhotoSpin/Artville; F77 (tr) PictureQuest, PhotoSpin/Artville; F78-9 (bkgd) ©VCG/FPG; F80-1 (bkgd) ©Richard Cummins/CORBIS; F81 (br) Richard Hutchings/Hutchings; F82 (b) Robert Holmgren/Peter Arnold, Inc.; F82 (t) ©Arthur Morris/Visuals Unlimited; F83 (bc) ©Rich Treptow/Visuals Unlimited; F83 (bcr) ©C.P. George/Visuals Unlimited; F83 (t) ©Barb Gerlach/Visuals Unlimited; F84 (br) Richard Hutchings/Hutchings; F85 (tr) Image courtesy of Barry Luokkala, Department of Physics, Carnegie Mellon University; F86 (b) Richard Hutchings/Hutchings; F87 (bl) Richard Hutchings/Hutchings; F87 (cr) Hutchings/Richard Hutchings; F87 (tr) ©Paul Silverman/Fundamental Photographs; F88 (bl) ©Roger Ressmeyer/CORBIS; F88 (inset) Roger Ressmeyer/Corbis; F88 (tc) Richard Hutchings/Hutchings; F88 (tcr) Richard Hutchings/Hutchings; F90 (tr) Cesar Llacuna/Cesar Llacuna; F91 Tony Freeman/PhotoEdit; F92 (bcr) North Wind Picture Archive/North Wind Pictures; F92 (br) Science Photo Library/Photo Researchers, Inc.; F92-3 (bkgd) Wolfgang Kaehler/CORBIS; F93 (bcr) The Schenectady Museum; F93 (br) The Queens Borough Public Library, Long Island Division,Latimer Family Papers/The Queens Borough Library/; F94-5 (bkgd) ©Jack Plekan/Fundamental Photographs; F95 (br) Richard Hutchings/Hutchings; F96 (b) Richard Hutchings/Hutchings; F96 (c) ©Alfred Pasieka/Science Photo Library/Photo Researchers, Inc.; F96 (t) ©Science/Visuals Unlimited; F97 (bcr) Richard Hutchings/Hutchings; F97 (bl) Richard Hutchings/Hutchings; F97 (t) ©Jeff Greenberg/Visuals Unlimited; F98 (bcl) Richard Hutchings/Hutchings; F98 (cl) Richard Hutchings/Hutchings; F98 (tr) ©Bill Beatty/Visuals Unlimited; F99 (bcl) Hutchings/Richard Hutchings; F99 (cl) Richard Hutchings/Hutchings; F100 (bc) Richard Hutchings/Hutchings; F100 (c) Richard Hutchings/Hutchings; F103 (cl) ©James Webb/PhotoTake; F107 (bkgd) ©Jeremy Walker/Stone Gettyone; F107 (br) Richard Hutchings/Hutchings; F109 (br) Hutchings/Richard Hutchings Photography; F109 (tr) Hutchings/Richard Hutchings Photography; F111 (br) McGraw-Hill School Division; F113 (br) ©Ed Degginger/Color-Pic, Inc.; F114-5 (bkgd) NASA Media Dallas; F115 (br) Ken Karp for MMH; F116 (b) Richard Hutchings/Hutchings; F117 (cr) n/a; F118 (inset) Bettmann/CORBIS; F119 (bcr) ©Hewlett Packard/Fundamental Photographs; F119 (inset) ©Hewlett Packard/Fundamental Photographs; F120 (br) ©1998 PhotoDisc, Inc.; F120 (inset) ©Science/Visuals Unlimited; F121 (tr) ©Carolyn A. McKeone/Photo Researchers, Inc.; F122 (bl) ©Science/Visuals Unlimited; F123 (tr) McGraw-Hill School Division.